INFORMATICS CURRICULA AND TEACHING METHODS

IFIP – The International Federation for Information Processing

IFIP was founded in 1960 under the auspices of UNESCO, following the First World Computer Congress held in Paris the previous year. An umbrella organization for societies working in information processing, IFIP's aim is two-fold: to support information processing within its member countries and to encourage technology transfer to developing nations. As its mission statement clearly states,

> *IFIP's mission is to be the leading, truly international, apolitical organization which encourages and assists in the development, exploitation and application of information technology for the benefit of all people.*

IFIP is a non-profitmaking organization, run almost solely by 2500 volunteers. It operates through a number of technical committees, which organize events and publications. IFIP's events range from an international congress to local seminars, but the most important are:

- The IFIP World Computer Congress, held every second year;
- Open conferences;
- Working conferences.

The flagship event is the IFIP World Computer Congress, at which both invited and contributed papers are presented. Contributed papers are rigorously refereed and the rejection rate is high.

As with the Congress, participation in the open conferences is open to all and papers may be invited or submitted. Again, submitted papers are stringently refereed.

The working conferences are structured differently. They are usually run by a working group and attendance is small and by invitation only. Their purpose is to create an atmosphere conducive to innovation and development. Refereeing is less rigorous and papers are subjected to extensive group discussion.

Publications arising from IFIP events vary. The papers presented at the IFIP World Computer Congress and at open conferences are published as conference proceedings, while the results of the working conferences are often published as collections of selected and edited papers.

Any national society whose primary activity is in information may apply to become a full member of IFIP, although full membership is restricted to one society per country. Full members are entitled to vote at the annual General Assembly, National societies preferring a less committed involvement may apply for associate or corresponding membership. Associate members enjoy the same benefits as full members, but without voting rights. Corresponding members are not represented in IFIP bodies. Affiliated membership is open to non-national societies, and individual and honorary membership schemes are also offered.

INFORMATICS CURRICULA AND TEACHING METHODS

IFIP TC3 / WG3.2 Conference on Informatics Curricula, Teaching Methods and Best Practice (ICTEM 2002) July 10–12, 2002, Florianópolis, SC, Brazil

Edited by

Lillian Cassel
Villanova University
USA

Ricardo A. Reis
Universidade Federal do Rio Grande do Sul
Brazil

KLUWER ACADEMIC PUBLISHERS
BOSTON / DORDRECHT / LONDON

Distributors for North, Central and South America:
Kluwer Academic Publishers
101 Philip Drive
Assinippi Park
Norwell, Massachusetts 02061 USA
Telephone (781) 871-6600
Fax (781) 681-9045
E-Mail <kluwer@wkap.com>

Distributors for all other countries:
Kluwer Academic Publishers Group
Post Office Box 322
3300 AH Dordrecht, THE NETHERLANDS
Telephone 31 78 6576 000
Fax 31 78 6576 254
E-Mail <services@wkap.nl>

 Electronic Services <http://www.wkap.nl>

Library of Congress Cataloging-in-Publication Data

A C.I.P. Catalogue record for this book is available from the Library of Congress.

Informatics Curricula and Teaching Methods
Edited by Lillian Cassel and Ricardo A. Reis
ISBN 1-4020-7266-X

Printed on acid-free paper.
Printed in the United States of America.

Contents

Foreword from the Program Chair   vii

Preface   ix

Conference Committees   xi

Acknowledgements   xiii

Benchmark Standards for Computing in the UK   3
  Andrew McGettrick

Student Experiments in Object-Oriented Modeling   13
  Torsten Brinda

Input/Output for CS1 Course in Java   21
  Elliot B. Koffman

Learning Programming by Solving Problems   29
  Amruth N. Kumar

Teaching of Programming with a Programmer's Theory of
Programming   41
  Juris Reinfelds

Teaching Programming Broadly and Deeply: The Kernel
  Language Approach   53
  Peter Van Roy, Seif Haridi

Programming Strategies using an Actor-Based Environment   63
    Raul Sidnei Wazlawick, Antonio Carlos Mariani

A Computing Program for Scientists and Engineers – What is   69
    The Core of Computing
    Ralf Denzer

Patterns of Curriculum Design   77
    Douglas Blank, Deepak Kumar

Variations in Computing Science's Disciplinary Diversity   87
    Luiz Ernesto Merkle, Robert E. Mercer

Variety in Views of University Curriculum Schemes for   97
    Informatics/Computing/ICT
    Fred Mulder, Karel Lemmen, Maarten van Veen

Reports of the Working Groups

Directions and Challenges in Informatics Education   115
    John Hughes, Andrew McGettrick, Ellen Francine Barbosa,
    Jens Kaasboll, Vinicius M. Kern, Ana Paula Ludtke Ferreira,
    Esselina Macome, Joberto Martins, Clara Amélia de Oliveira,
    Alfonso Ignacio Orth, R. Sadananda, Elaine da Silva,
    Romero Tori

Teaching Programming and Problem Solving   125
    Elliot Koffmann, Torsten Brinda, Juan Alvarez, Amruth Kumar,
    Maria Lucia B. Lisboa, Juris Reinfelds, Peter Van Roy, Raul
    Sidney Wazlawick

Computing: The Shape of an Evolving Discipline   131
    Lillian Cassel, Gordon Davies, Deepak Kumar, Ralf Denzer,
    Anneke Hacquebard, Richard LeBlanc, Luiz Ernesto Merkle,
    Fred Mulder, Zeljko Panian, Ricardo Reis, Eric Roberts, Paolo
    Rocchi, Maarten van Veen, Avelino Francisco Zorzo

Author Index   139

Foreword from the Program Chair

ICTEM 2002 follows a tradition of working conferences held every one or two years under the auspices of IFIP Working Group 3.2, which addresses issues related to teaching informatics and using information and computing technology at the university level. The ICTEM 2002 conference was organized around three themes:

1. Directions and challenges in informatics education.
2. Teaching programming and problem solving.
3. Informatics: One discipline or many?

The invited participants were partitioned into three working groups, one for each theme, and each working group produced a report that is intended to provide a summary of current issues and future directions relative to its theme. Most conference participants also presented a paper related to one of the themes.

The discussions and paper presentations during the conference were productive and interesting. The working groups did an excellent job of producing reports after only a few, but very intensive, working group sessions during the conference. The conference venue was a delightful beach-side setting near Florianópolis, Brazil, and the conference took place July 10-12, 2002. It is hoped that the selected papers and the working group reports that are provided here will be a useful resource in future developments related to informatics education at the university level.

Joe Turner
ICTEM 2002 Program Chair

Preface

This book contains a selection of the papers presented at the IFIP WG 3.2 Working Conference on Informatics Curricula, Teaching Methods and Best Practice – ICTEM 2002, plus three reports from the groups that worked during the conference. ICTEM2002 took place at the Jurerê Beach Village Hotel, in Florianópolis Brazil, from 10 to 12 July 2002.

The 13 papers selected to be included in this book were chosen from 24 papers presented at the conference. These papers report on several aspects of informatics curricula and teaching methods such as:

- Challenges in Defining an International curriculum
- The diversity in informatics curricula
- Computing programs for scientists and engineers
- Patterns of curriculum design
- Student interaction
- Teaching of programming
- Peer review in education

The working group meetings were organized in three parallel tracks. Working Group 1 discussed the "Directions and Challenges in Informatics Education". The focus of Working Group 2 was "Teaching Programming and Problem Solving". Working Group 3 discussed "Computing: the shape of an evolving discipline." Each WG worked actively and prepared a report with the results of the discussions; these reports are included as the second part of this book. The success of the conference format and themes discussed encourage the participants to work on organizing new meetings to continue the work on informatics curricula.

We hereby would like to thank IFIP and more specifically IFIP WG 3.2, the Brazilian Computer Society and ACM for the support of this event. We also would like to thank the participants who contributed to the success of the conference, the reviewers who carefully selected and provided feedback for the papers and the conference organizers who have done a great job.

Lillian N. Cassel
Ricardo Reis
Co-editors

July 2002

Conference Committees

Program Committee

Joe Turner, USA **(Program Chair)**

Bob Aiken, USA

Boots Cassel, USA **(Co-Editor)**

Daltro José Nunes, Brazil

Gordon Davies, United Kingdom

John Hughes, Australia

Raul Sidnei Wazlawick, Brazil **(Organizing Chair)**

Ricardo Reis **(Co-Editor)**

Roberto Bigonha, Brazil

Wilfried Brauer, Germany

Organizing Committee

Aldo von Wangenheim

Edla Maria Faust Ramos

Fernando Alvaro Ostuni Gauthier

Frederico Agenor Alvares

Maria Marta Leite

Murilo Silva de Camargo

Jorge Muniz Barreto

Jovelino Falqueto

Raul Wazlawick, Brazil **(Organizing Chair)**

Roberto Willrich

Rogério Cid Bastos

Silvia Modesto Nassa

Acknowledgements

This book is the result of the work of many dedicated volunteers: conference chairs, session organizers and moderators, program committee, authors of papers, conference staff and the sponsors. We thank all of them for their contribution and particularly to Raul Waslawick, Organizing Chair of ICTEM and Dayane Montagna, head of the conference secretariat.

INFORMATICS CURRICULA AND TEACHING METHODS

Benchmark Standards for Computing in the UK

Andrew McGettrick
Department of Computer and Information Sciences; University of Strathclyde; Glasgow, Scotland
andrew@cs.strath.ac.uk

Abstract: In the UK the Government is concerned that standards should exist to ensure that all degrees awarded in institutions of higher education meet certain minimal criteria and therefore are of at least of a certain standard. To this end they have created a set of committees composed of subject experts whose task is to define the required standards for their discipline. The purpose of this paper is to outline the approach taken to address these benchmarking standards for Computing.

Key words: computing education, curriculum standards

1. BACKGROUND

Document [1] laid the foundations for the discussion and debate on benchmarking standards. This led to the formulation by the UK Quality Assurance Agency (QAA) of a requirement for experts to produce benchmarking standards for their discipline, i.e.

> *to produce broad statements which represent general expectations about standards for the award of honours degrees in a particular subject area. Benchmarking is not about listing specific knowledge, that is a matter for institutions in designing individual programmes. It*

is about the conceptual framework that gives a discipline its coherence and identity; about the intellectual capability and understanding that should be developed through a the study of that discipline to honours degree level; the techniques and skills which are associated with developing an understanding in that discipline; and the level of intellectual demand and challenge which is appropriate to honours degree study in that discipline.

This report describes particular aspects of the benchmarking standards for the discipline of Computing. It was produced by a Committee selected jointly by the Conference of Professors and Heads of Computing (CPHC) and the British Computer Society (BCS) as being representative of a broad range of discipline expertise from within the UK. See [2].

2. THE TASK

Within the academic community a wide range of terms are used to describe degrees in the subject area. Computer science, computing science, computing, software engineering, software technology, information systems, artificial intelligence, computer systems engineering and information engineering are among the more common. Indeed the Committee had to provide benchmarking standards that would accommodate in excess of 2,400 different courses. The Committee took the view that the naming of degrees would be the responsibility of individual institutions and accordingly the standards should relate to the discipline and not just degrees with specific titles.

In producing the document, the Committee was conscious of the need to involve the academic community but also to take advice from the professional bodies (including the British Computer Society, the Institution of Electrical Engineers, the Software Engineering Association, the Academy of Information Systems and the AISB) and generally from industry and commerce as well as the public. Accordingly, a wide-ranging consultation process was used to confirm that the balance and the thrust of the document reflected agreed-upon views. Moreover, throughout the development of the standards it was deemed important to keep the academic community informed of developments as they unfolded. A web site was set up to inform interested parties.

3. AUDIENCE

The final Benchmarking Standards document had to meet the needs of four particular groups at least. These were the academic reviewers who would carry out reviews of departments, the general public who wish to be informed about the discipline, course developers, and finally external examiners. The manner in which the Committee set out to address these needs is given below.

3.1 Academic Review

Ultimately this process of academic review would involve an assessment of each Computing department in the UK; academic reviewers would have to make judgements about whether degree courses met the standards and had to be given guidance on how to address these benchmarking standards

3.2 The Public

To be accessible to a wide audience the standards had to be couched in language that was non-technical and non-threatening; yet, it was important to convey the sense of a new and exciting discipline that had the potential to open up a wide range of possibilities for study and future career opportunities

3.3 Course Developers

To stimulate the design and development of new and imaginative courses the Committee included a section on diversity of course provision; in addition, the standards were phrased in a manner intended to encourage novelty and not to constrain unduly

3.4 External Examiners

For this group (who as visitors to departments would have to agree to and preside over the awards of degrees) it was decided that guidance would be provided in terms of what should be sought, for example, in reviewing examination papers, in looking at final year projects, in guidelines that might apply for examination boards and so on. It was specifically not the intention that the benchmarking standards would be used when considering, for example, the award to each individual student

4. ISSUES

A variety of issues caused the Committee a great deal of debate. Below five of these are highlighted.

4.1 Title of Discipline

Originally the Committee had been charged with producing benchmarking standards for the discipline of Computer Science. Consultation with the community produced an overwhelming reaction to the title and asked that this be changed to Computing. This change occurred.

4.2 Rate of Change

Given the nature of the discipline, and the rapid developments that are causing regular changes to the curriculum and the method of teaching, it is to be expected that curricula in Computing will have to change on a regular basis. To address this, the benchmarking standards were written without reference to specific details of today's technologies. In the longer term the benchmarking statements themselves would need to be reviewed. For those undertaking any revision, the thinking of the initial committee would be relevant. Accordingly, a rationale document was produced. More generally, it was hoped that all the academic community would find this of value since it provides insight into the processes that underlie everything to do with benchmarking activity.

4.4 Considerations on Core Content

In considering the issue of course design, one central concern was whether there should be core material that would be common to all courses. To include a core would tend to constrain thinking and to limit diversity. Yet, there is some very basic material that surely everyone should know. In exploring thoughts in this area, it appeared that this material was largely either

- skills based, and could be captured under the heading of IT skills, or
- it related to the crucial areas of requirements, specification, design, implementation, maintenance.

Indeed this was the approach used.

4.5 Body of Knowledge

In their deliberations, the committee produced a body of knowledge that was intended to outline the breadth of the discipline. There was great debate about what role, if any, this should play. Should it appear in the main text, should it be an annex, should it be present at all? In the end, the Body of Knowledge appears as an Annex. But, the concerns of the committee, i.e. that this would be interpreted as curricula, remain a concern.

4.6 Benchmarking Standards

The QAA had insisted only that the committee articulate a set of criteria for threshold levels. This was to be interpreted as the gaining of an honours degree. The committee felt that, in the interests of the public perceptions of the subject and encouraging excellence, this alone would not reflect the best interests of the discipline. Accordingly, a decision was made to define modal standards also and to make comments about requirements that should apply for the best students.

5. TOWARDS BENCHMARKING STANDARDS

In considering their remit, the committee felt that it should set out a number of fundamental aims and objectives, which could then guide their thinking.

5.1 Basic Considerations

Computing should be presented as a discipline in which -teaching and learning was characterised by a blend of knowledge (including underpinning as well as the principal methods and methodologies), understanding, practical work, appreciation of applications and attitudes. Practical activity should reflect a disciplined approach that includes a careful blending of skills underpinned by theory as well as the application of methods and methodologies, and the use of tools in support of these applications.

Within courses, there should be encouragement for creativity and innovation, as well as active learning. Assessment should reflect this as well as a problem solving approach. Courses must be up-to-date (students are viewed as agents of technology transfer) in terms of content (practices of the subject including skills) and equipment (software, hardware, communications, etc.). Courses need also to be relevant to the modern world and include attention to communications skills, teamwork, IT and numeric skills as well as life-long learning. In addition, there should be an element of flexibility to address student choice, especially in the later stages of a course.

5.2 Characteristics of Benchmarking Standards

Benchmarking Standards in Computing would have to

- accommodate a wide variety of courses
- capture the essence of Computing, and present a consistent philosophy about the nature of the discipline
- take account, where appropriate, of the engineering ethos, and provide no conflict with accreditation criteria
- encourage innovation and creativity in course provision, as well as better courses
- ensure up-to-date provision, and take account of the needs of industry (and be relevant)

In addition they should

- accommodate modular provision, joint courses, etc.
- be meaningful, accommodate levels and ideally be succinct
- reflect student achievement (and include attention to progress rates)
- accommodate assessment against standards which must be straightforward and unambiguous

By contrast, the benchmarking standards in Computing should *not*

- be technology dependent or date quickly
- lead to national curricula
- limit diversity or stifle the development of new courses
- confuse accreditation and quality assessment which are different
- favour one kind of approach, e.g. hardware or software, formal or informal, highly theoretical
- be bureaucratic or create revolution
- relate purely to difficulty or to the purely academic.

6. FINAL REPORT

6.1 Structure

In the end, the structure of the Benchmarking Standards document was as follows:

1.	The Study of Computing
2.	The Curriculum
2.1	The cognate area
2.2	Abilities and skills
3.	Course design
3.1	Principles of course design
3.2	Themes
3.3	Diversity of provision
4.	Learning, teaching and assessment
4.1	Learning and teaching
4.2	Student motivation
4.3	Student induction
4.4	Assessment issues
4.5	Learning environments and resources
5.	Benchmarking standards
5.1	Threshold
5.2	Modal
Annex A	Body of Knowledge

6.2 Commentary

It seemed inadvisable to separate out teaching and learning from assessment. The maxim that 'assessment guides learning' is particularly apposite in this regard. Consequently, the three topics of teaching, learning and assessment are grouped together and addressed within the one section.

In outlining a number of knowledge areas and skills to be acquired, the committee were conscious of the possible adverse affects of a large assessment load.   Novel ways had to be found of countering such developments and, as a result, section 4.4 raises the concerns and encourages novel ways of addressing the issues.

In the same vein, the committee took the view that student motivation is a very important matter and likewise student induction; the latter implies conditioning the expectation and providing guiding. The implication is that there should be an expectation that departments would need to address these important matters.

A final comment here relates to the issue of whether the standards are demanding. Certainly for traditional Computer Science degrees, for instance, there will be an expectation of a mathematical underpinning, a rigorous approach, appropriate attention to the usual design skills and professional attitudes, as well as experience of conducting a major project. The section on themes states

> *Courses need to be designed to possess themes that ensure students are equipped to contribute to the development of major components of computer systems in a manner that ensures they are fit for the purpose for which they were intended.*

It is important to remember that these benchmarking standards are minimal standards to be reached by all honours degree courses.

6.3 Illustration

To illustrate the resulting standards, the modal standards are reproduced below. It should be noted that there are additional requirements, e.g. the existence of themes within the body of knowledge to ensure depth, attention to the lifecycle phases (of requirements, specification, etc.), attention to professional and ethical issues, the acquisition of certain skills and so on. Within that context, the following is illustrative of certain key features.

6.3.1   Modal standard

Students reaching this will be able to:

– demonstrate a sound understanding of the main areas of the body of knowledge within their programme of study, with an ability to exercise critical judgement across a range of issues;

- critically analyse and apply a range of concepts, principles and practices of the subject in an appropriate manner in the context of loosely defined scenarios, showing effective judgement in the selection and use of tools and techniques;
- produce work involving problem identification, the analysis, the design and the development of a system, with accompanying documentation. The work will show problem solving and evaluation skills, draw upon supporting evidence and demonstrate a good understanding of the need for quality;
- demonstrate transferable skills with an ability to show organised work as an individual and as a team member and with minimum guidance;
- apply appropriate practices within a professional and ethical framework and identify mechanisms for continuing professional development and life long learning;
- explain a wide range of applications based upon the body of knowledge.

7. FINAL REMARKS

The main test of these benchmarking standards will occur when they are used 'in anger', i.e. to carry out assessments of individual departments. This has now happened and the feedback is positive. Indeed, they have now been used to guide benchmarking activity in other disciplines and they also form the basis of revised accreditation criteria as used by the UK professional bodies.

A new activity is now about to commence, namely the difficult task of benchmarking Masters courses in Computing.

8. ACKNOWLEDGEMENTS

The work reported here owes everything to the ideas and contribution of the other members of the Benchmarking Panel, namely John Arnott, David Budgen, Peter Capon, Gordon Davies, Peter Hodson, Elizabeth Hull, Gillian Lovegrove, Paul McGrath, Keith Mander, Arthur Norman, Stanley Oldfield, Vic Rayward-Smith, Anne Rapley, Dan Simpson, Aaron Sloman, Frank Stowell and Neil Willis.

9. REFERENCES

[1] The Report of the National Committee of Inquiry into Higher Education, chaired by Lord Dearing, published by HMSO, London, 1997.
[2] Computing, Benchmark Standard published by the UK Quality Assurance Agency, Gloucester, England, 2000

Student experiments in object-oriented modeling

Torsten Brinda
Department of Didactics of Informatics
University of Dortmund
44221 Dortmund Germany
e-mail: torsten.brinda@udo.edu

Abstract   Exploration modules (EMs) and structures of knowledge as essential components of the author's concept "Didactic system for object-oriented modelling (OOM)" for improving the OOM education are introduced as new learning aids for student-centered learning. The didactic criteria "Basic concepts on different abstraction levels" and "Synchronization, transformation and evaluation of views" for the design of EMs are developed. A methodology for designing a "didactic map" of object-oriented basic concepts as a process oriented learning aid is described. The activities of learners when using EMs with the solution of complex problems, e.g. modelling a library system, are illustrated. The strategy for inclusion in the Informatics teacher education is connected with some words on the concepts' efficiency.

1. MOTIVATION

Good career prospects in the Informatics field led to an enormous increase in the number of Informatics study beginners at German universities from the middle of the nineties. According to the German Federal Office of Statistics, the total number of Informatics study beginners (first university semester) has risen steadily from 4611 in 1995/96 to 11496 in 1999/2000. The Informatics faculties can hardly cope with this crowd. For example, in the semester 2000/01 the University of Dortmund had to schedule lectures repeatedly per week due to the entry of about 1100 beginners. The load on students and lecturers was enormous. According to information from the German "Fakultätentag Informatik" (steering committee of all accepted German Informatics faculties) the ratio of graduates in relation to study beginners has fallen from 50% in 1999 to 45% in 2002. This reflects an increase in the number of university dropouts and also in the study length of students. There is a need for a change in the study processes. In the year 2001, the German Ministry of Education and Research started to support about 100 university collaborative research projects in the field "New Media in Higher Education". About a fourth of these projects were Informatics projects. Multimedia e-learning materials were developed to support student-centered learning and to relieve overburdened Informatics faculties. The work of consortia like the "European Consortium of Innovative Universities" [4] extends this approach to an international level.

Besides the development and distribution of e-learning materials, the Informatics study must be developed further by including new learning forms and learning aids so that student-centered learning, self- paced learning, and the preparation for lifelong learning become essential structuring elements of the learning process. Learning concepts, which should be taken into account in this context more strongly, include active and explorative learning [5, p. 150]. Traditional learning scenarios in higher Informatics education do not include enough such natural learning forms. An auditorium is a difficult environment for learning by discovery. Within the approach of "discovery learning" the teacher should design the learning process as a sequence of problem situations, each involving a learning task, which stimulate the learners' research interest. Suitable result-oriented learning aids are necessary to support learners in their explorative learning process.

Brinda and Schubert developed a concept called "Didactic system for object-oriented modelling" as a combination of traditional and new studying concepts [2, 3, 7]. The concept addresses beginners in object-oriented modeling (OOM), selected for the study because of its relevance in a variety of Informatics areas such as software engineering and object-oriented databases. The main goal of the didactic system is to bring a new quality of learning to the OOM field. The didactic system makes it possible for learners to navigate in structures of knowledge, to construct solutions for exercises from exercise classes, and to learn by discovery with exploration modules (EMs). In the context of this paper, EMs can be thought of as software modules (small applets, applications and animations). In a wider sense, learning texts and other media are included to form more complex EMs. Here the main emphasis lies on structures of knowledge and the embedding of EMs in the social process of Informatics study. Exercise classes are discussed in [2].

2. EXPLORATION MODULES AS NEW LEARNING AIDS

Discovery learning strategies are often applied by Informatics students as a work reduction strategy. They discover and then reuse standard algorithms from textbooks. The same strategy is used with software libraries. Available solution parts are adapted and integrated in the solution of new problems to avoid repeated development. This intrinsic motivation, which lies within the subject, led to the concept of the EMs. Learners explore EMs in suitable learning scenarios and in that way learn about basic object-oriented concepts and object-oriented models.

Within the design of EMs, manipulative and perceptive ways of exploration have to be considered. Manipulative exploration allows the exploring person to change something and get immediate feedback. The EM has to provide specific manipulation and observation components, combined with check mechanisms. Perceptive exploration requires structures that can be discovered. Therefore, the EM has to offer multiple cognitive approaches, which show the explored object in different ways and combine or even synchronize different views to visualize complex structures. By didactic analysis of the OOM field indicates that beginners should get to know and design structures (static basic concepts) and understand and control processes (dynamic basic concepts). Starting from an application they should analyze, modify, construct, and assess object-oriented models in the stages of structure element, structure, and model. This results in the exploration promoting features of EMs shown in table 1.

Table 1. Exploration promoting features of EMs

Feature	Description
Basic concepts on different abstraction levels	Structures, their elements and models must be explorable on different abstraction levels to give learners with various pre-knowledge a cognitively demanding entry to object-orientation, i.e. the complexity of views ought to be adjustable. It has to be possible to switch on or off selected views. For beginners as a minimum of one static view (class diagram) and one dynamic view (interaction diagram) are necessary to describe the structure and the time change of an object-oriented model.
Synchronization, transformation and evaluation of views	Synchronization represents a "didactic bridge" between different diagrams. This makes it possible to bring the single views together to a picture of the complete system and to overcome a known cognitive barrier. For some educational purposes, it should be possible to synchronize different views automatically. If learners do this manually, model check functions must be provided to prove the model's consistency.

In the study year 2001/2002 the author was leader of a student project group which developed EMs as a "Learning Environment for Object-oriented modeling – LEO". At the University of Dortmund the "project group" is a compulsory course for advanced Informatics students. For two semesters and 16 hours per week, eight to twelve Informatics students work in a team on the solution of a large programming task. The collection of EMs, which the group developed, is based on the features discussed before. Within LEO, learners can select "scenarios", e.g. "mobile communication" or "library". In traditional learning processes, it is hardly possible to discuss all solutions discovered by the learners. EMs can help in that more learners get individual feedback. In section 3 the inclusion of EMs in the study process will be discussed with concrete examples.

2. DEVELOPMENT OF A DIDACTIC MAP

Discovery learning results in a qualified structure of knowledge Not very much is known about the process of its development. A didactic map is a process-oriented learning aid on which individual exploration paths between concepts can be marked. The map provides better orientation in and self organization of the learning process. . The didactic map is also helpful for learners to reflect on and to assess their individual knowledge construction [1].

Table 2. : Procedure of development of the didactic map for object-oriented basic concepts

Phase	Activities
1. Construction of a list of OOM concepts	Analysis of textbooks, journals, internet resources on OOM and extraction of typical concepts
2. Filtration of the concept list	Definition and application of didactic selection criteria: *Affiliation to OOM*: Concepts, which do not belong to the OOM core e.g. memory principles, are removed. *Redundancy*: Only one representative of synonymous concepts remains in the list. *Generic terms*: Generic terms are preferred to specializations. *Language specificity*: Language specific concepts are removed. *Relevance*: Concepts without relevance for the target group are removed.
3. Structuring of the concept list	Identification of concept classes and sub classes in the list (e.g. object, class, variable, method, relationship, diagram) and classification of the concepts of the list
4. Visualization as a mindmap	Visualization of the structure and the neighborhood relationships within the list as a mindmap
5. Transformation of the mindmap to a didactic map	Mapping of classes to continents, subclasses to states and concepts to cities and description of possible connections between concepts of different quality as e.g. roads or highways

Phase	Activities
6. Connecting the map with EMs	Provision of EMs, which allow discovery of neighbored concepts, each in one area of the map
7. Discovery journeys through the lands of OOM	Planning of discovery journeys within the lands of OOM Technical support by colorization mechanisms that indicate which areas have already been visited

The analogy between structures of knowledge and a map is useful: neighbored concepts can be connected with roads, learning barriers can be visualized, for example as rivers and hills. A more formal mode of didactic maps called "And-Or-Graphs" has been introduced in [2]. The explication of the relationships between concepts stimulates learners to build up their own structures of knowledge by using EMs, which help them acquire a set of covered concepts by exploration. Depending on the phase of the learning process, a didactic map can be given by the teacher or be developed in the team. Beginners, who need orientation in the learning process, will be given a version of the didactic map to see which EMs cover which parts of the map. Advanced learners can refine and enhance a given map or develop new ones to explicate their structures of knowledge.

Within the scope of the LEO project a didactic map has been developed for the field of object-oriented basic concepts. In table 2 the procedure of its development is described. Educational phases, which make this possible, are designed as a discovery process to promote the learners' individual knowledge construction. The teacher requires the structuring of the individual findings of the learners and their connection with the theory of object-oriented modelling. Learners are not left alone with their problems; they become integral an element of the discussion. This concept is suitable for exercises, seminars, and traineeships;, but in the context of notebook universities, it is also suitable for lectures.

3. INCLUSION IN THE STUDY PROCESS

An explorative approach is not a trial-and-error strategy. The learner's ability to form a hypothesis is sharpened, because with the help of EMs they build up hypotheses that they later refute or validate. This requires the discussion of systematic exploration strategies as well as basic knowledge of OOM.

Torsten Brinda

In the example case, the first aim of the learners was to simplify the work processes in a library with an informatics system. Previous knowledge of the learners consisted of the static- and dynamic basic concepts of OOM and the script language Python. The learners work with EMs, which support the exploration of models and process steps within the library example. They transfer their findings about model elements and the construction of model views onto their own designs and the models thus take on a tactical role [6]. An EM provides a possible textual specification of the library system and identifies object, class, method, attribute, and relationship candidates within

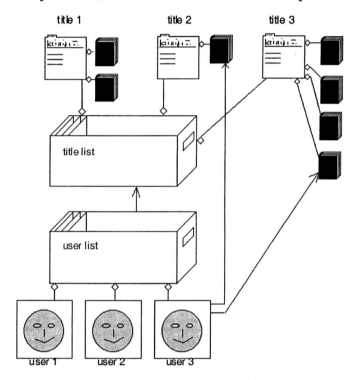

Figure 1: LEO - object view of the library scenario

the text by application of text based heuristics. The learners explore steps of a process model, which results in a first version of a class diagram. They rediscover the concept of inheritance with the example of the two similarly structured lists: titles and users. In the class view, the EM therefore inserts an abstract list class as a super class over the specialized list classes. At first, the list class does not contain any attributes or methods. That allows learners to "move" suitable attributes along the inheritance relationships. To understand how system objects cooperate in the final library system in order to realize the system aim, an EM is provided that visualizes the usually hidden message exchange. Starting from a class diagram learners instantiate objects and construct an object diagram (figure 1). They then check whether an object diagram is consistent with a class diagram.

In the object diagram, they invoke methods of the objects, observe and check the state changes and simulated message exchange between the objects. Accompanying to the explorative phases, the group constructs solution parts of the library problem in the team. Assumptions of the learners regarding the problem specific objects, attributes, and methods are collected and systemized in the team.

In the following, each learner selected a field for which he or she wanted to design an informatics system. They proceed strategically because they identify the problems and rediscover methods with EMs to solve them. The learners work on their chosen problems and construct a class diagram and a sequence diagram for each essential method. Here the change and the combination of model views play an important role. To become aware of the consideration of consistency and completeness of models, the learners use an EM with which they construct class and sequence diagrams for their models. On demand, the EM checks the consistency and indicates missing model elements (e.g. missing methods in the class diagram or contradictory signatures of methods) based on the constructed models. The learners evaluate these reports and understand how completeness and consistency can be achieved. Logical mistakes or missing classes cannot be identified by the EM. The learners present their results, analyse and discuss them with ,other students. The evaluation of this reflection helps them with the solutions of their own problems. Moreover, the learners select and apply EMs of the library example to refresh their knowledge about the interplay of the different views. A better picture of the relationship of static and dynamic models is achieved, which the learners transfer to their own problems.

EMs have a pedagogical double function because they can be learning aids as well as the lesson object. Advanced learners analyse EMs and their development documentation (analysis, design, and source code documents). Successful structuring ideas are identified and generalized within the group. The learners reflect these findings and include them in the solution of their own problems. In project groups, they can also develop new EMs, which will be used as learning aids for following student generations.

The concept "Didactic System for object-oriented modelling" has proven its success in a number of fields. It has been used successfully at the University of Dortmund for the education of student teachers of Informatics [3]. In several in-service training sessions for Informatics teachers in Germany as well as in Denmark the author received positive feedback. Materials distributed within the author's departmental electronic library (http://ddi.cs.uni-dortmund.de/iml/) were praised by German Informatics teachers. These materials have also been used successfully for a lecture called "Introduction to Informatics for arts scholars". The underlying development concept has successfully been adapted for a German government project and a European project on e-learning.

4. BIOGRAPHY

Torsten Brinda was born in 1972. He received his diploma in computer science from the University of Dortmund (Germany) in 1998. In 1998 he became assistant professor in Didactics of Informatics at the University of Dortmund. From 1999 to 2001 he was manager of a multimedia project in teacher education. From 2001 to 2002 he was the leader of the LEO project. His research interests are concepts for e-learning and learning and teaching object-oriented modelling in secondary- and higher education. In 2001 he received the "best paper award" of the German national conference on "Informatics and School – INFOS2001".

5. REFERENCES

[1] Anderson, J. R. (1995) Cognitive psychology and its implications. W. H. Freedman and Company, New York.

[2] Brinda, T.; Schubert, S. (2002a) Didactic system for object-oriented modelling, in *The seventh World Conference on Computers in Education (WCCE2001)*, Post Conference Proceedings, Kluwer Academic Publishers, Boston, in press.

[3] Brinda, T, Schubert, S.: (2002b) Learning aids and learners' activities in the field of object-oriented modelling, in *The seventeenth World Computer Congress (WCC2002)*, Post Conference Proceedings, Kluwer Academic Publishers, Boston, in press.

[4] European Consortium of Innovative Universities – ECIU. 2002. http://www.eciu.org/.

[5] Turner, A. J. (1998) Trends in teaching informatics, in *Informatics in Higher Education* (ed. F. Mulder and T. van Weert). Chapman & Hall, London, 148-155.

[6] van Weert, T. (2001) Co-operative ICT-supported learning. A practical approach to design, in *Informatikunterricht und Medienbildung* (ed. R. Keil-Slawik and J. Magenheim, J.). Köllen, Bonn, 47-62.

[7] Vygotsky, L. S. (1978) Mind in Society. Harvard University Press, London.

Input/Output for a CS1 Course in Java
Some Considerations

Elliot B. Koffman
Computer and Information Science Department, Temple University, Philadelphia, PA, USA
koffman@temple.edu

Abstract: This paper discusses considerations for input/output for a first course in Java. It includes the opinions of several computer science educators regarding the pros and cons of using a non-standard package for input/output and the requirements of such a package. It also describes the evolution of a simple package for input that it is easy to implement using the Swing class and gives guidelines for using standard Java for simple input/output.

Key words: Computer Science 1 (CS1), Novice programming in Java

1. INTRODUCTION

1.1 Non-standard packages for input/output

Many Java textbooks for CS1 use simple packages for Java input/output. Some classes that were developed to simplify console input/output are: ConsoleReader [3], Text [2], and SimpleInput [1]. These classes were written because the textbook authors and teachers of CS1 recognized that console-based input in Java is difficult for novices to use. At the same time, a few packages were also written that permitted GUI-like interactivity. Examples of these packages and classes are: simpleIO [7] and Java Power Tools [8]. These packages were developed because their implementers recognized that console-based input/output was tedious and uninteresting to students who were accustomed to applications with Graphical User Interfaces (GUIs). The package developers also felt that novice students should be able to write programs with GUI-like interactivity before mastering the Java APIs that would enable them to build their own GUIs: AWT and Swing.

1.1.1   Educator comments on using non-standard packages

In early April, 1999 there was a thread on the SIGCSE listserve that discussed the use of non-standard packages for teaching CS1 in Java. The messages seemed to be split fairly evenly between those who advocated their use and those who were against their use. The following comment by H. Conrad Cunningham (University of Mississippi) succinctly summarizes the two points of view:

"On one hand, use of simplified I/O or GUI packages can make Java easier to teach and use in CS1/CS2. So the various packages that are available with various textbooks can be helpful. And we want to convey to our students that it is easy to add on significant capabilities to Java and other such languages.

On the other hand, there is concern that use of a non-standard, add-on package might be confusing to first year students. Students tend to take what they learn as being part of Java. When they move to another environment, they are somewhat lost and confused. They have the overhead of relearning an I/O package or installing the one they are accustomed to. There is thus some sentiment to only teaching the "standard" (whatever that means with Java)."

A. Joseph Turner (Clemson University), makes the following point in favor of using packages:

"I haven't tried teaching CS1 or CS2 using only the classes in the standard Java library, but unless you want to limit yourself to reading only a character at a time or a line at a time (as a string), you don't want to use only the I/O facilities in standard Java. (There are some ways to do a bit better than reading only characters or lines, but the overhead and complexity of doing so are out of the question for beginning students as far as I am concerned.)"

David Arnow (Brooklyn College of City University of New York) makes the following argument against the use of packages:

"There is another argument in favor of NOT providing a special I/O package for student use in CS1/Java. While constructions such as

```
BufferedReader br = new BufferedReader(
                new InputStreamReader(
                new FileInputStream(
                new File("myinput"))));
```

may be introduced as "boilerplate", they also provide an opportunity to:

– emphasize the idea of classes as models, as repositories of particular sets of behavior.
– illustrate the use of composition
– foster the notion and UTILITY of abstraction

In connection with the latter, students, even CS1 students, can appreciate the fact (and the accompanying discussion) that the last two lines of the above code can be replaced with

System.in

or

new URL("http://www.acm.org").openStream()));

or

all sorts of other things eventually

because each of these things play the "role" of an InputStream. In other words, if one's goal is to take an object-oriented approach in CS1 Java's I/O classes can be viewed as an asset, not a liability. (As a side note, this i/o stuff usually turns out to be the LEAST of the students' problems in CS1.)"

Michael G. Branton (Stetson University) advocates teaching basics of the AWT first instead of using packages:

"You can also do it with Java without that much fuss. I've taught the course 3 times now using AWT. you don't need very much of it to put a text field or 2 and a button on the screen, folks. There seems to me a lot of hand-wringing over this, but I've found that my students don't find this difficult to deal with at all. It's the algorithm development that's still the "hard part." My experience is that teaching them enough of the GUI for CS1 doesn't take much time at all. I still have plenty of room for the topics I consider important, and text fields and buttons give them something very concrete (in a virtual sort of way :-)) to think of as objects right off the bat."

Finally, Judy Bishop (University of Pretoria) makes the following points in favour of non-standard packages:

– "Java is an extensible language, with extensions coming via packages (APIs). In today's world, the ability to harness this power is more integral and more important for fresh minds to understand in *week one*, than a long-winded object instantiation, four brackets deep.
– An I/O class is an excellent case study in its own right as it illustrates exception handling, as well as tokenizers and string functions. It also does not have to be long: our Text class is 2.5 book pages of code, providing 10 methods for input, output and file opening.
– If a lecturer feels very strongly about teaching Java at the rock face, and is not convinced by point 1, then I would still suggest that when writing your own package! comes along in the course (which it ought to at some stage), then an I/O or Graph package is an ideal candidate."

What have we learned from this thread?

1. There are rather strong opinions about the pros and cons of using packages.
2. If authors or teachers wish to use a package, they should think of the package as "training wheels" to give a student the feel for programming with GUIs in Java without the overhead of learning the AWT (or Swing) from the start.
3. Because the package will be discarded, it should be relatively easy to learn how to use it.
4. The package should be fairly easy to implement, so students have little difficulty understanding it as a case study.

2. EVOLUTION OF A PACKAGE FOR USER INPUT

In earlier papers [5, 8], Koffman and Wolz, described two packages for user interactivity in a Java course. The first, simpleIO [8], contained a class SimpleGUI with instance methods for displaying dialog windows and menus for user input. Class SimpleGUI also had instance methods for incorporating user interactivity in graphics programming and for simplifying file input/output. Finally, it provided as "output" a history of all user interaction with objects that extended class SimpleGUI. Class SimpleGUI was not easy for a beginner to use because a class performing input/output operations needed to instantiate SimpleGUI or extend it in order to call its methods. Also, it was not easy to implement and understand SimpleGUI because it was designed using the Java 1.0 AWT class. For these reasons, SimpleGUI did not meet criteria 3 and 4 in the paragraph above.

The second package [5] was more modest in its goals. It enabled novice programmers easily to display dialog windows for input, including menus. It also enabled students to display windows with simple messages, or to display text areas containing several lines of output. All methods are static methods, so there is no need to instantiate a class or to extend it. Also, all methods are relatively easy to implement (between 5 to 15 lines each), so the package can be used as a case study.

The input class KeyIn provides methods readChar(), readDouble(), readInt(), and readString(), which display a dialog window and return a data value of the type indicated by the method name. For example, the statement

```
int pennies =
          KeyIn.readInt("Enter the count of pennies");
```

displays the dialog window in Figure 1 and returns as its result the integer value (155) typed in by the user. For readChar(), readInt(), and readDouble(), if the user enters an item that is not the required data type, an error window appears (see Figure 2). After the user presses OK, the dialog window reappears and the user has another chance to enter a valid data value. Also, the user can also restrict the range of values by supplying additional arguments:

```
int pennies =
    KeyIn.readInt("Enter the count of pennies", 0, 100);
```

If the user enters an out-of-range value, an error window appears (see Figure 3) and the user is prompted again to enter a valid data item. Methods readChar(), readDouble(), readInt() call method showInputDialog() of Swing's JOptionPane class to display dialog windows, and they call method showMessageDialog() to display error message windows.

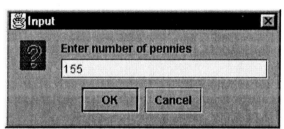

Figure 1. Dialog window for integer data

Figure 2. Error message for invalid data

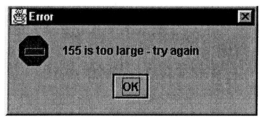

Figure 3. Error message for out-of-range data

Method readBoolean() enables a student to display a window with buttons labels "Yes" (for true) and "No" (for false). The statement

```
boolean mood = KeyIn.readBoolean("Are you happy");
```

displays the dialog window show in Figure 4.

Method readChoice() enables a student to display a menu and returns an integer corresponding to the button pressed by the user. The statements

```
String[] coffeeChoices = {"Rain Forest", "Decaf",
                          "Expresso", "Latte"};
int myCoffee = KeyIn.readChoice("Select a coffee",
                          coffeeChoices);
```

display the menu window shown in Figure 5 ("Rain Forest" is 0, "Latte" is 3).

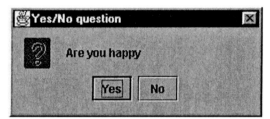

Figure 4. Reading a Boolean value

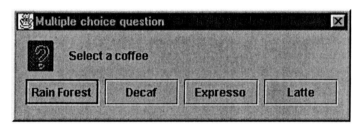

Figure 5. A Simple Menu

A companion class, UserOut, has a method displayResult() that displays its argument string in a message window. For multiple line output, method appendOutput() enables a student to append output lines to a text area. Method displayOutput() displays the text area in a window. Method clearOutput() clears the text area. The statements below fill and display the text area shown in Figure 6.

```
for (int i = 0; i < 3; i++) {
  int next = KeyIn.readInt("next number");
  UserOut. appendOutput( "next number is " + next);
}
UserOut.displayOutput();
```

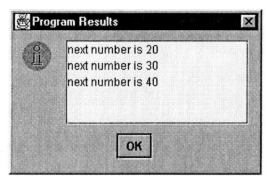

Figure 6. Output window with text area

3. A MORE CONSERVATIVE APPROACH TO I/O

After presentation of a paper describing this package at ACM SIGCSE [5], the author began to rethink the advisability of using a non-standard class for performing output. The output methods of class UserOut do not provide sufficient benefit beyond what is available in standard Java 2.0 to offset the overhead of teaching students how to use these methods and later abandoning them when GUIs are introduced. Students can call JOptionPane's method showMessageDialog() to display a string in a message window. Since it is desirable to teach students how to use the Java console window for debugging, students can also use the Java console window to display multiple line program output instead of using an output text area.

Although a non-standard package is still useful for input, it is reasonable and feasible to teach students how to call the methods of class JOptionPane directly. This would enable some faculty to restrict their students to standard Java if they wished, but would enable others to simplify their students' code with a non-standard package. This approach also ensures that students who use the package would understand how to implement its methods using standard Java.

As an example, the first statement below

```
String penniesStr = JOptionPane.showMessageDialog (
                    null, "Enter the count of pennies");
int pennies = Integer.parseInt(penniesStr);
```

displays the dialog window shown earlier in Figure 1; the second statement converts the data item entered by the user (a string) to an integer that is stored in pennies. Unfortunately, an invalid data item would raise an exception that would cause the program to terminate because the code does not catch invalid numeric data. Students can write simple static methods that provide the same functionality as shown next.

```
public static int readInt(String prompt) {
   String xStr =
      JOptionPane.showMessageDialog(prompt);
   int xVal = Integer.parseInt(xStr);
   return xVal;
}
```

The standard Java call to method showConfirmDialog() below displays the Yes/No dialog window shown earlier in Figure 4. The assignment statement stores true or false in variable mood. Similarly, students can call showOptionDialog() to display a menu (Figure 5) and return a type int result.

```
int happyNum = JOptionPane.showConfirmDialog(null,
                                 "Are you happy?");
boolean mood = (happyNum == 0);
```

4. SUMMARY

The paper describes instructors' attitudes towards using non-standard packages for input/output in a first course in Java and some guidelines for developing and using such packages. It describes the evolution of such a package. Because the package is easy to implement and understand, it can be used as a case study to illustrate design techniques and to help students understand new Java concepts. The paper also describes a simple approach to using standard Java for input/output in which the console window is used for program output and dialog windows are used for input.

5. REFERENCES

[1] Barnes, D. J., Object-Oriented Programming with Java, Prentice Hall, Upper Saddle River, NJ, 2000.

[2] Bishop, J., Java Gently, Addison-Wesley Longman, Essex, England, 1997.

[3] Horstmann, C., Computing Concepts with Java 2 Essentials, Second Edition, John Wiley & Sons, New York, NY, 2000.

[4] Koffman, E., and Wolz, U., Problem Solving with Java, First Edition, Addison Wesley, Reading, MA, 1999.

[5] Koffman, E., and Wolz, U., A Simple Java Package for GUI-like Interactivity, Proceedings of 32nd Annual SIGCSE Symposium, February, 2001, 11-15.

[6] Koffman, E., and Wolz, U., Problem Solving with Java, Second Edition, Addison Wesley, Reading, MA, 2002.

[7] Raab, J., Rasala, R., and Proulx, V. K. Pedagogical Power Tools for Teaching Java, SIGCSE Bulletin, 32(3), 156-159.

[8] Wolz, U. and Koffman, E., simpleIO: A Java Package for Novice Interactive and Graphics Programming, SIGCSE Bulletin, 31(3), 139-142.

Learning Programming by Solving Problems

Amruth N. Kumar
Ramapo College of New Jersey; 505, Ramapo Valley Road; Mahwah, NJ 07430-1680
amruth@ramapo.edu

Abstract: We have been developing tutors to help students learn programming concepts by solving problems. In this paper, we will discuss the use of problem-solving in Computer Science, the effectiveness of using problem-solving tutors to learn programming concepts, and the pedagogical relationship between solving problems and learning to write programs. We will also present the design and results from the evaluation of one of our tutors.

1. PROBLEM-SOLVING AND COMPUTER SCIENCE

Problem-based learning improves long-term retention [12], and is better than traditional instruction for improving the ability of students to solve real-life problems. In Computer Science, various researchers have advocated the use of self-paced exercises [24], practice to build problem-solving skills [35], and the use of frequent, graded assignments in a course [9]. It is reported that "students universally want to see more examples both in class and in their textbooks" [38]. Solving problems facilitates active learning, whose place in Computer Science education has been established [26].

Textbooks are generally inadequate as sources of problems because of their limited, non-interactive nature. Even in disciplines such as Physics and Mathematics, where textbooks generally tend to include many more practice problems than in Computer Science, faculty are increasingly turning to the use of technology to address this issue. Typically, programs are written to generate problems, and such programs are made available to students for practice, e.g., CAPA [16] for Physics, and CHARLIE [4] for electronics and control systems. Kashy [17] reports that the use of such programs has increased student performance by 10%, largely due to increased time spent on the task.

Different types of problem-solving tutors have been developed for Computer Science topics that provide students with frequent, self-paced exercises:
– Numerous systems demonstrate the solving of *problems entered by the student* - JFLAP [33] for Automata Theory and PSVE/GAIGS [27] for parameter passing mechanisms are two representative examples.
– Numerous algorithm animation and visualization systems (e.g., JHAVE [28], JAWAA [32]) *generate data* to animate algorithms.
– Some systems *administer problems* generated by the instructor. These include WebToTeach [2], APMS [18], WebCT (www.webct.com), and other such course administration systems.
– A few systems have been developed to *generate problems* for students to solve: PILOT [7] for graph algorithms, Gateway Labs for problems in mathematical foundations of Computer Science [3], and SAIL [8], which is a LaTeX-based scripting tool for problem generation.

Few, if any systems have been developed to help students learn programming by solving problems, wherein the systems themselves generate problems for the students to solve. Two reasons for this may be:
– Programming problems are not quantitative (vis-à-vis say, Physics or electronics). Instead, they depend on the structure of arbitrary programs, which are hard to generate automatically.
– Computer Science educators have traditionally considered the norm for student practice to be a small number of large programming exercises in a course, rather than a large number of small practice problems. However, education research indicates that focused practice (such as solving problems) is just as important for learning as contextualized and expansive projects (such as whole language approach in reading instruction) [25,14,10]. In other words, students must solve problems about specific programming constructs just as much as write comprehensive programs to build their programming and problem-solving skills.

5. PROBLETS: PROBLEM-SOLVING TUTORS FOR COMPUTER SCIENCE

We have been developing problem-solving tutors, called problets, for selected programming concepts. These tutors are capable of generating problems, grading the student's solution, providing immediate and detailed feedback about the correct answer, logging the student's performance, and determining whether the student has learned the material.

- **Problem Generation:** The problets generate an endless supply of problems on a specific topic, by randomly instantiating problem templates encoded into them in pseudo-BNF notation by either the problet designers or the instructor using the problet.
- **Problem Solving:** The problets are capable of solving the problems they generate. The answers to the problems need not be encoded into the problets.
- **Providing feedback on User's Answers:** The problets provide feedback at two levels: at the minimal level, they correct the user's answer; at the detailed level, they also explain the correct answer.
- **Grading User's Answers:** The problets report whether the user's answer is correct, incorrect or partially correct. They keep score for the user, and are capable of terminating a session when the user has reached a preset level of proficiency in the topic.

The effectiveness of using problem-solving tutors has been well documented in literature:

- The field of *Intelligent Tutoring Systems*, which is the basis of our solution, has documented an improvement of one standard deviation through the use of tutors [1].
- The use of similar tutors has been shown to increase student performance by 10% in Physics [17].
- Our own work in building and testing tutors for Computer Science has shown that the *average* performance in a class improves by 100% after using the tutor [19], [20], and that the improvement is systemic [37].

The tutors are designed to promote active learning. They target **application** in Bloom's taxonomy of educational objectives [5], and are expected to supplement the traditional programming projects assigned in the course, which emphasize **synthesis**. Since research indicates that focused practice such as that provided by the tutors is just as important for learning as large-scale projects [25], so we expect the use of tutors to complement the traditional programming projects.

To date, we have developed, deployed and assessed tutors on several programming topics, including expression evaluation in C++ [19], pointers for indirect addressing in C++ [20], nested selection statements in C++ [36], static scope in Pascal [21,22] and parameter passing in programming languages [37]. We also plan to build a series of tutors for most of the imperative programming constructs covered in a typical *Computer Science I* course, and evaluate the effectiveness of using them to improve retention in the course. Our tutors may be used not only for practice solving problems, but also for assignments and tests. The tutors are delivered over the Web, so they can be accessed any time, anywhere.

2. FROM SOLVING PROBLEMS TO WRITING PROGRAMS

Learning to program involves both learning to design and write programs, and learning to read and understand programs. Whereas the focus of introductory Computer Science courses is in general the former, i.e., learning to design and write programs, the importance of the latter cannot be over-emphasized. Computer Science students must learn to read and understand programs because professional programmers must often cooperate with others to write programs, and may have to maintain software written by someone else.

Learning to read and understand programs may contribute to a student's ability to, in turn, design and write programs:
- **Active Effect:** Students generate mental models when reading programs, which may in turn help them visualize solutions when writing programs;
- **Passive Effect:** Students have to read their own programs in order to debug/test them. Since debugging/testing is a part of the write-compile-debug-test cycle of program development, any improvement in the ability to read and understand programs helps students write programs more efficiently.

Solving problems to learn programming could involve either writing programs or analysing given programs. Since students already write programs as part of class assignments, the focus of our tutors is on analyzing given programs. The problems generated by our tutors engage the learners in one of two analytical activities: debugging the presented program, or predicting the output of the program. This helps students learn by examples, both good and bad. These activities promote the students' ability to read and analyze programs written by them as well as others.

The program comprehension model developed by Pennington [29,30] investigated the detailed mental representations formed by programmers studying programs written in the imperative style. It was derived from models of text comprehension developed and refined over the years [15,34,39]. Pennington's model of program comprehension includes the following two layers, which are progressively more abstract:

– **Program Model**, which consists of knowledge of operations carried out in source code, and control flow - low level details that are localized and explicitly available in the program text.
– **Domain Model**, which consists of knowledge of data flow and the goals that a program accomplishes – abstract details that are distributed and implicit in a program. It is difficult to understand programs when related data transformations are carried out in non-contiguous segments of code [23].

Pennington found that novice programmers built a strong program model, but a weak domain model after studying imperative programs written in FORTRAN, COBOL and Pascal [11], whereas expert programmers built a stronger domain model than novice programmers. Pennington argues that the performance of comprehension-demanding tasks is likely to play an important role in the formation of domain model, which is built slowly in the context of meaningful programming tasks. Program debugging and prediction of output are comprehension-demanding tasks presented by our tutors. Hence, our tutors may be said to promote the development of a stronger domain model among novice programmers. In general, our tutors address both problem domain (e.g., expression evaluation, code with syntax errors) and domain model (dangling pointers, scope issues, lost objects, memory-out-of-bounds, semantic errors, etc.).

Theorists have identified three levels of learning [14,10,40], through which novice learners progress: emergent stage, when they are first exposed to the task; developing stage, when they recognize patterns and begin using appropriate tools; and transitional stage, when they carry out the tasks increasingly correctly, despite incomplete understanding and an initial lack of confidence. Our tutors can be used in all the above stages: with detailed feedback during the emergent stage, with minimal feedback during the developing stage, and without any feedback during the transitional stage.

3. EVALUATION OF PROBLETS

Our tutor on C++ pointers presents C++ programs and asks the user to indicate whether the program contains any dangling pointers, lost objects, semantic errors (printing values of un-initialized variables), syntax errors, etc. We have evaluated this tutor in several sections of our *Computer Science II* course. In this section, we will present the results of these evaluations, addressing both cognitive and affective aspects of learning with the tutor.

3.1 Cognitive Learning with the Problet

Tutor in Isolation: In Fall 2000, we tested the tutor in two sections (N=19 combined), by administering a pretest, followed by practice using the tutor, and a post-test. These were not controlled tests. The author was the instructor in both the sections. The pre-test and post-test scores were out of 40. The results are presented in the Table below.

Table 3. Tutor in Isolation

(N=19)	Pre-Test	Post-Test	Effect Size
Average	12.21	26.74	2.16
Std-Dev	6.70	8.73	

The Effect Size is calculated as (post-test score - pretest-score) / standard deviation on the pre-test. An effect size of 2.16 sigma indicates that the tutor facilitated learning among the students. The improvement is statistically significant (2-tailed $p < 0.05$). It compares favourably with the result that individual human tutors can bring students 2 sigma above normal classroom instruction [6].

Tutor Versus Printed Workbook: In Spring 2001, we again tested the tutor in two sections (N=33 combined), using the pretest-practice-posttest protocol. We conducted a controlled test – between the tests, the control group practiced with printed workbooks, whereas the test group practiced with the tutor. The author was not the instructor in the sections. The pre-test and post-test scores were out of 40. The results are presented in the Table below.

Table 4. Tutor vs Printed Workbook

(N=33)	Pre-Test	Post-Test	Effect Size
Tutor Users			
Average	13.00	23.06	1.52
Std-Dev	6.61	10.12	
Workbook Users			
Average	15.24	24.71	1.33
Std-Dev	7.10	10.54	

Practicing with the tutor appeared to be slightly better than practicing with the printed workbook. Both the improvements were statistically significant (2-tailed $p < 0.05$).

Minimal Versus Detailed Feedback in the Tutor: In Fall 2001, we conducted a controlled test of the tutor in two sections (N=22). This time, we tested two versions of feedback for the tutor: minimal versus detailed. In minimal feedback, the tutor corrects the user's answer, but does not explain the correct answer. In detailed feedback, in addition, the tutor explains the correct answer. We used the same pre-test-practice-post-test protocol as before, with fixed times for each step. Incorrect answers were penalized. The author was not the instructor in either class. The pre-test and post-test scores were out of 80. The results are presented in the Table below.

Table 5. Minimal vs detailed feedback in the tutor

	Pre-Test	Post-Test	Effect Size
Detailed Feedback (N=14)			
Average	11.57	27.29	1.99
Std-Deviation	7.91	21.01	
Minimal Feedback (N=8)			
Average	8.25	17.38	1.63
Std-Deviation	5.60	14.62	

The results seem to indicate that detailed feedback may be better than minimal feedback. For detailed feedback, the 2-tailed $p < 0.05$, indicating that the improvement is statistically significant, whereas $p = 0.28$ for minimal feedback, indicating that the improvement is not statistically significant.

3.2 Affective Learning with the Problet

Students filled out a feedback form after the controlled tests in Spring 2001, in which they provided feedback about the instrument they had used for practice between pre-test and post-test (workbook for control group and tutor for test group, N=33). These feedback forms clearly indicate that the tutor facilitates affective learning. On a Likert scale of 1 (Strongly Agree) to

5 (Strongly Disagree), the average scores of the test and control groups on the questions of the feedback form are as shown in the table below.

Table 6. Student feedback

Feedback Question (Test Group: Instrument = Tutor; Control Group: Instrument = Printed Workbook)	Tutor Users	WorkBook Users
1. It was easy to (learn to) use this instrument.	2.13	2.29
2. The problems posed by the instrument were clear.	1.94	1.94
3. The instrument listed interesting problems.	2.13	2.35
4. The problems were repetitive and boring.	3.44	3.06
5. The instrument provided useful feedback.	2.20	3.06
6. The instrument helped me learn the material.	2.31	2.88
7. Using this instrument was time-consuming.	3.88	3.12
8. The instrument should be made available to all students	1.56	2.65
9. If this instrument is made available, I will use it	1.93	2.65
10. I would like to see such instruments on other topics.	1.44	2.59

Question 1 indicates that the tutor was easy to learn if we use the control group's score as the basis, since presumably, students do not need to "learn" how to use a printed workbook designed like a typical textbook. The problems in the printed workbook were themselves generated by the tutor, and the results for Question 2 validate this. Questions 3 and 4 seem to indicate a slight Hawthorne effect in that students using the online tutor felt the problems were more interesting and less repetitive and boring, although the types of problems were the same for both the tutor and the printed workbook. Question 5 clearly indicates the superiority of the tutor, which provided detailed problem-specific feedback whereas the printed workbook just listed the correct answer for each problem. Questions 6 and 7 indicate that the tutor facilitated better affective learning than the printed workbook, which is encouraging. Questions 7 through 10 clearly indicate the students' preference for the tutor over the traditional printed workbook.

4. FUTURE WORK

It is clear from the improvement from pre-test to post-test scores, that students learn how to solve problems using our tutors. We would like to test whether this improvement in problem-solving ability translates to better ability to write programs.

Pennington [29] found that a cross-referenced mental representation, containing a balanced mix of program and domain model is associated with better program comprehension. She also found that modification tasks promoted the development of a cross-referenced mental representation. Our tutors currently do not ask the users to modify the programs, only to debug or predict their output. We may include program modification as another activity in our tutors in the future.

Self-generated elaborations are better than text-supplied elaborations for learning [31]. In other words, if the user is provided with an environment in which the user can construct his/her own explanation for a program, the user will benefit more than if the tutor generates all the explanations. It would be an interesting exercise to incorporate this meta-cognitive reasoning into our tutors. Since the problem (code segment), solution and feedback are all textual in our problets, they favor verbal learners over visual learners in the Felder-Silverman Learning Style model [13]. We would like to address the needs of visual learners by incorporating program animation into our problets.

5. ACKNOWLEDGMENT

Partial support for this work was provided by the National Science Foundation's Course, Curriculum and Laboratory Improvement Program under grant DUE-0088864.

6. REFERENCES

[1] Anderson, J.R., Corbett, A.T., Koedinger, K.R., Pelletier, R. "Cognitive Tutors: Lessons Learned". *The Journal of the Learning Sciences*. Vol 4(2), 167-207, 1995.

[2] Arnow D. and Barshay, O., WebToTeach: An Interactive Focused Programming Exercise System, In proceedings of FIE 1999, San Juan, Puerto Rico (Nov. 1999), Session 12a9.

[3] Baldwin, D., Three years experience with Gateway Labs, Proceedings of ITiCSE 96, Barcelona, Spain, June 1996, 6-7.

[4] Barker, D.S., CHARLIE: A Computer-Managed Homework, Assignment and Response, Learning and Instruction Environment, *Proc. of FIE 1997*, Pittsburgh, PA (Nov. 1997).

[5] Bloom, B.S. and Krathwohl, D.R. Taxonomy of Educational Objectives: The Classification of Educational Goals, by a committee of college and university examiners. Handbook I: Cognitive Domain, NewYork, Longmans, Green, 1956.

[6] Bloom, B.S.: The 2 Sigma Problem: The Search for Methods of Group Instruction as Effective as One-to-One Tutoring. *Educational Researcher*, Vol 13 (1984) 3-16.

[7] Bridgeman, S., Goodrich, M.T., Kobourov, S.G., and Tamassia, R., PILOT: An Interactive Tool for Learning and Grading, *Proceedings of the 31st SIGCSE Technical Symposium*, Austin, TX, (March 2000), 139-143.

[8] Bridgeman, S., Goodrich, M.T., Kobourov, S.G., and Tamassia, R., SAIL: A System for Generating, Archiving, and Retrieving Specialized Assignments Using LaTeX, *Proc. of the 31st SIGCSE Technical Symposium,* Austin, TX, (March 2000), 300-304.

[9]   Campbell, J.O., Evaluating Costs and Benefits of Distributed Learning, Proceedings of FIE 1997, Pittsburgh, PA (November 1997).

[10] Calkins, L., The Art of teaching writing, Heinemann, 1986.

[11] Corritore, C.L. and Widenbeck, S. What do Novices Learn During Program Comprehension? *Intl. Journal of Human-Computer Interaction*, 1991, 3(2), 199-222.

[12] Farnsworth, C. C., Using computer simulations in problem-based learning. In *Proc. of Thirty Fifth ADCIS conference*, Omni Press, Nashville, TN, (1994), 137-140.

[13] Felder, R., Reaching the Second Tier: Learning and Teaching Styles in College Science Education. *Journal of College Science Teaching*. 23(5): 286-190, 1993.

[14] Holdaway, D., The Foundations of Literacy, Heinemann, 1980.

[15] Johnson-Laird, P.N. Mental Models: Towards Cognitive Science of Language, Inference and Consciousness. Cambridge University Press, Cambridge, 1983.

[16] Kashy, E., Sherrill, B.M., Tsai, Y.., Thaler, D., Weinshank, D., Engelmann, M., and Morrissey, D.J., CAPA, An Integrated Computer Assisted Personalized Assignment System, American Journal of Physics, Vol 61(12), 1993, 1124-1130.

[17] Kashy E., Thoennessen, M., Tsai, Y., Davis, N.E., and Wolfe, S.L. Using Networked Tools to Enhance Student Success Rates in Large Classes. In *Proceedings of FIE '97* (Pittsburgh, PA, November 1997), IEEE Press, Session T3A.

[18] Kohne, G.S., An Autograding (Student) Problem Management System for the Compeuwtir Illittur8, Proceedings of ASEE Annual Conference, June 1996 (CD ROM).

[19] Krishna A. and Kumar A. A Problem Generator to Learn Expression Evaluation in CS I and Its Effectiveness. *Journal of Computing in Small Colleges*, Vol 16(4), 2001, 34-43.

[20] Kumar A. Learning the Interaction between Pointers and Scope in C++, *Proceedings of The Sixth Annual Conference on Innovation and Technology in Computer Science Education (ITiCSE 2001)*, Canterbury, UK, (June 2001), 45-48.

[21] Kumar A.: Dynamically Generating Problems on Static Scope, Proceedings of The Fifth Annual Conference on Innovation and Technology in Computer Science Education (ITiCSE 2000), Helsinki, Finland, (July 2000), 9-12.

[22] Kumar, A, Schottenfeld, O. and Obringer, S.R. Problem Based Learning of 'Static Referencing Environment in Pascal, *Proc. of the 16th Annual Eastern Small College Computing Conference (ESCCC 2000)*, University of Scranton, PA, (Oct 2000), 97-102.

[23] Littman, D.C., Pinto, J., Letovsky, S., and Soloway, E. Mental Models and Software Maintenance. In E. Soloway and S. Iyengar (Eds.), *Empirical Studies of Programmers*, 1986, Ablex Publishers, Norwood, NJ, 80-98.

[24] Liu, M.L., and Blanc, L., On the retention of female Computer Science students, *Proc. of the 27th SIGCSE Technical Symposium*, Philadelphia, PA, March 1996, 32-36.

[25] Mann, P., Suiter, P., and McClung, R., A Guide for Educating Mainstream Students, Allyn and Bacon, 1992.

[26] McConnell, J., Active Learning and its use in Computer Science, Proceedings of ITiCSE 96, Barcelona, Spain, June 1996, 52-54.

[27] Naps, T.L., and Stenglein, J., Tools for Visual Exploration of Scope and Parameter Passing in a Programming Languages Course, The Proceedings of 27th SIGCSE Technical Symposium on Computer Science Education, February 1996, 305- 309.

[28] Naps, T.L., Eagan, J.R.. and Norton, L.L. JHAVE – An Environment to Actively Enhage Students in Web-Based Algorithm Visualizations. *Proceedings of the 31st SIGCSE Technical Symposium*, Austin, TX, March 2000, 109-113.

[29] Pennington, N. Comprehension Strategies in Programming. G.M. Olson, S. Sheppard and E. Soloway (Eds.), *Empirical Studies of Programmers: Second Workshop*, Ablex Publishers, Norwood, NJ, 100-113, 1987.

[30] Pennington, N. Stimulus Structures and mental Representations in Expert Comprehension of Computer Programs. *Cognitive Psychology*, 19, 295-341, 1987.

[31] Reder, L., Charney, D., and Morgan, K. The Role of Elaborations in Learning a Skill from Instructional Text. *Memory and Cognition*. 14: 64-78, 1986.

[32] Rodger, S., JAWAA, 1997, http://www.cs.duke.edu/~rodger/tools/tools.html

[33] Rodger, S., and Gramond, E., JFLAP: An Aid to Study Theorems in Automata Theory, Proceedings of ITiCSE 98, Dublin, Ireland, August 1998, 302.

[34] Schmalhofer, F. and Glavonov, D. Three Components of Understanding a Programmer's Manual: Verbatim, Propositional and Situtational Representations. *Journal of Memory and Language*, 1986, 25, 295-313.

[35]`Schollmeyer, M., Computer Programming in Highschool versus College, Proceedings of the 26th SIGCSE Technical Symposium, Philadelphia, PA, February 1996, 378-382.

[36] Singhal N., and Kumar A., "Facilitating Problem-Solving on Nested Selection Statements in C/C++", *Proc. of FIE '00*, Kansas City, MO, October 2000, IEEE Press.

[37] Shah, H. and Kumar, A., "A Tutoring System for Parameter Passing in Programming Languages", *Proc. of The 7th Annual Conference on Innovation and Technology in Computer Science Education (ITiCSE 2002)*, Aarhus, Denmark, (June 2002), 170-174.

[38] Tilbury, D., and Messner, W., Development and Integration of Web-based Software Tutorials for an Undergraduate Curriculum: Control Tutorials for MATLAB, Proceedings of FIE 97, Pittsburgh, PA, November 1997.

[39] Van Dijk, T.A. and Kintsch, W. Strategies of Discourse Comprehension. Academic Publishers, New York, 1983.

[40] Vygotsky, L., Mind in Society: Development of Higher Psychological Functions, Harvard University Press, 1978.

Teaching of Programming with a Programmer's Theory of Programming

Juris Reinfelds
Klipsch School of EE & C,
New Mexico State University
Las Cruces, NM, USA
juris@nmsu.edu

Abstract: We review the introductory programming courses of the widely accepted Curricula '68, '78, '1991 and '2001. We note that a one-language, imperative-paradigm approach still prevails, although multi-language programming systems are already available. We discuss the Kernel Language Approach, which provides a programmer's theory of programming that permits a widening of introductory courses to multi-language, multi-thread programming without loss of depth. We suggest two broad outlines for the removal of the one-language constriction from introductory programming courses. We observe that because of the introduction of dotNET and because of student exposure to net-centric multimedia applications, text-based "Hello World !" examples disappoint the expectations of today's students.

Key words: programming methodology, programming courses, curriculum, computer science, software engineering, introductory courses,

1. INTRODUCTION

In order to make progress, we first divide and conquer and then we unify [1]. In the sixties scientific programming was done in FORTRAN, commercial data processing was done in COBOL and algorithms were supposed to be programmed in an "algorithmic language" called ALGOL. These three language groups did not speak to each other much, went to separate conferences, did not read each other's publications. Soon each developed its own style of programming and the notion of *programming paradigms* was born.

Excessive originality was highly praised, especially in academia, which adopted the algorithmic language branch, and created the important functional, logical and object-oriented paradigms as well as an endless stream of "new" programming languages. In 1969 [3] Jean Sammet described 120 reasonably widely distributed programming languages in her book. She maintained a yearly register of programming languages for the first half of the seventies, where we can see how casually new programming languages were proclaimed and how quickly they were forgotten.

As a new science trying to gain respect among older, well-established sciences, computing needed a theory in a hurry. Mathematicians had elegant theories of computability, developed when hand computations by mathematicians were the only way to compute. Computer science adopted them, gained respect and "forgot" that computer programmers work with a very different set of concepts than hand-calculating mathematicians or mathematicians who are interested in the foundations of computability.

2. PROGRAMMING IN THE CURRICULUM

ACM Curriculum'68 [2] was the first widely accepted curriculum for undergraduate Computer Science. It combined programming with problem solving in a 3-credit-hour lecture-plus-laboratory course:

2.1 B1 – Introduction to Computing

"... a **single** algorithmic language should be used for most of the course... It may be desirable to use a **simple second** language of quite a different character for a problem or two to demonstrate the wide diversity of computer languages available..."

The suggested course material for B1 was very extensive, so that the next ACM Curriculum'78 [4] split it into two 3 credit-hour lecture-plus-laboratory courses that "forgot" about the second language suggestion of B-1

2.2 CS-1 Computer Programming

"... introduce problem solving methods and algorithm development... ...teach **one** high level programming language that is widely used... ...teach how to design, code, debug and document programs..."

2.3 CS-2 Computer Programming II

"...continue development of discipline in program design...   ...introduce basic aspects of string processing, recursion and simple data structures..."

Curriculum'78 also had a course on programming languages and their implementation that was based on I-2 of Curriculum'68:

2.4 CS-8 Organization of Programming Languages

"...develop understanding of organization of programming languages and their run-time behaviour..."

The focus on one programming language created by Curriculum'68 and reinforced by Curriculum'78 started a heated debate as to which language should be *the chosen one*, a debate that continues today. A glance at the program of the most recent ACM SIGCSE'2002 conference [5] shows two sessions on CS-1 and one session on CS-2 where the question *"Which language will give us the quickest and best understanding of programming?"* still dominates.

3. RECENT CURRICULA

IEEE-CS joined with ACM to create Computing Curricula 1991 [6] which did not question the one-language approach and retained CS-1 and CS-2 as *"Introduction to Computing I and II"*, while CS-8 became *"Programming Languages"* with emphasis on a feature by feature comparison of major programming paradigms. The language implementation part of CS-8 was dropped into a course on compilers.

The most recent Computing Curricula'2001 [7] acknowledged that a consensus on "the chosen language" or even "the chosen paradigm" has not been reached and is not likely. Instead, Curricula'2001 introduce a gaggle of introductory courses entitled Imperative first, Object first, Functional first, Breadth first, Algorithms first and Hardware first, that are otherwise very similar to CS-1 and CS-2. The Programming Language course suggested by Curricula'2001 retains the "comparison of language features" character of CS-8.

Although we now have to solve problems with scope and size that were unthinkable twenty years ago, nothing much has changed in the programming curricula since 1968 and 1978. As Peter Van Roy remarks in his paper in this conference [8]

"...programming is taught as a craft in the context of a single paradigm ... often explicitly limited to a particular language and toolset. Almost no attempt is made to put these tools into a uniform framework."

4. A PROGRAMMER'S THEORY OF PROGRAMMING

A *programmer's theory of programming* should explain programming in terms of concepts that are already familiar to programmers. A *theory of programming* should capture the essence of programming and place a unifying foundation under programming languages.

The first programmer's theory of programming was developed by Edsger W. Dijkstra [9]. Dijkstra introduced the notion of "guarded statements" and captured the essence of imperative programming with a very small set of well-chosen and precisely defined statements. Precise semantics were defined using Boolean expressions as pre-conditions, post-conditions and loop invariants. Dijkstra's theory was very useful for the creation of easily understood programs for difficult algorithms [9], [10], [11].

5. THE MULTI-PARADIGM PROGRAMMING LANGUAGE OZ

Is it possible to design a programming language that is equally expressive, but much smaller and more elegant than the union of all programming language features from all paradigms? The Oz programming language [12] answers the question with a resounding yes.

Can such a language be implemented reliably and efficiently on multiple platforms? The Mozart [12] system gives us an implementation of Oz, a compiler, a runtime environment and program development tools that are outstanding in every respect.

Without direct knowledge of how it actually happened, we can guess that the designers of Oz first extracted the essence of each paradigm. Then they devised a syntax and semantics that combine these essentials into one precisely defined programming language. Finally they added some "syntactic sugar" which are statements that increase the expressivity of the programmer and the readability of the program.

One way to keep a combination of several things small is to look for commonalities that were overlooked before. For example, in the heyday of esoteric mainframes, each operating system was an independent creation influenced by the underlying hardware, but even more by the exuberant creativity of its designers.

Then came UNIX that captured the essence of an operating system by stating that everything that stores information is a *file* and everything that manipulates information is a *process*. The hardware and software implementation of files and processes were left to hardware and software designers. Programmers could reason about operating system behaviour without resorting to implementation arguments and the first multi-platform system was born.

Oz bases the essence of programming languages on values and threads. A *value* is either simple (e.g. integer, float, procedure ...) or structured (e.g. array, record, list ...). A *thread* is an executing statement-sequence. A new, concurrent thread, which runs in parallel with the thread that creates it, may be created with the simple statement

thread <any statement sequence> end

Moz maintains a global name-space of unique internal names of variables that permits a simple variable-scope-rule:

> For all threads, remote as well as local, all variables that are in scope when a thread-statement executes, remain available during execution of the thread body, regardless of termination of the parent thread execution.

In other words, variable scopes do not change when a statement sequence is executed in its own thread. The run-time system makes values available to processes that need them in a transparent and efficient way.

By contrast, Java language designers placed the burden of remote-thread variable resolution on Java programmers and Java run-time implementers added to the programmer's burden the proper placement of "synchronized" tags on selected methods.

To accommodate declarative programming and to facilitate reasoning about multi-thread programs, Oz uses assign-once-only (like final variables of Java) variables as the primary variables. For programming with state, Oz provides cells, which are assign-many–times variables.

6. THE KERNEL LANGUAGE APPROACH

Compared to its multi-paradigm, distributed and concurrent programming scope, Oz is a surprisingly compact language. Nevertheless, Van Roy and Haridi [13] went a step farther and defined a subset of Oz that captures the essence of Oz in a remarkably small and elegant syntax and operational semantics. Every statement of Oz can be reduced to statements of this subset. Hence they named the subset *"A Kernel Language of Oz"*. Since Oz spans the major paradigms as well as multi-thread computing, we expect that this Kernel Language will provide a basis for most programming languages as discussed by Van Roy and Haridi [13], where they extend the Kernel Language approach to the programming languages Erlang, Haskell, Java and Prolog.

There is one more level of structure. The Kernel Language has a very small declarative core that we may regard as the basic foundation of programming. With small extensions of the core Van Roy and Haridi [13] create Kernel Languages for the bases of other paradigms and for concurrent and distributed computing.

7. IMPACT OF KERNEL LANGUAGE ON INTRODUCTORY COMPUTER SCIENCE TEACHING

From Curriculum'68 to Curricula'2002, three courses, CS-1, CS-2 and ProgLangs have been allocated to the teaching of programming. CS-1 and CS-2 were tied to one programming language. This has not changed to this day.

Artificial boundaries of programming paradigms prevent students from seeing programming as a unified whole. The first "chosen language" FORTRAN was replaced by BASIC, which was replaced by Pascal, which was replaced by C, which C++ tried to replace and which is being replaced by Java. Curriculum'68 [2] had great foresight when it tried to tie its Programming Languages course to

> "... a survey of the significant features of existing programming languages with particular *emphasis* on the *underlying concepts* abstracted from these languages..."

but without a programmer's theory of programming there was no coherent set of underlying concepts and the course degenerated into a descriptive comparison of programming language features [14].

There have been some attempts to overcome the one-language syndrome of CS-1 and CS-2. None have survived mainly due to faculty reluctance to master more than one programming language, program development environment and compiler.

With National Science Foundation support in 1992 and 1993, we developed a laboratory-based three-paradigm CS-1, CS-2 course sequence [15], [16], with Prolog, Miranda and C representing the logical, functional and imperative paradigms. Students enjoyed the course, but faculty, support staff and teaching assistants did not. The mastering of three unrelated program development environments and compilers took too much time and energy away from the programming focus of the courses.

With the multi-paradigm, multi-thread language Oz and a Kernel Language with which we can define and discuss the essence of each paradigm as well as concurrent and distributed computing in simple, yet precise terms, we finally have the missing theory of programming with which we can reorganize CS-1, CS-2 and ProgLangs to teach more material, achieve better depth of understanding and reach more students than with the current suggestions of Curricula'2002 which simply continue the approach of Curriculum'68 and '78.

Included below are two suggestions at the two ends of the student mind-set spectrum of how we can improve CS-1, CS-2 and ProgLangs with the help of the Kernel Language Approach.

8. INTRODUCTORY CURRICULUM FOR SERIOUS STUDENTS

Serious students want a deep understanding of programming concepts as soon as possible. Serious students are not comfortable with the use of black-box components and large, opaque subprogram libraries. They are not happy with having to click-select menu-items more or less at random to see "by experiment" whether the item fits into the program. Instead they like to reason about and clearly understand program statements and components before they use them in their programs. This suggests the following three courses

8.2 CS-1

Introduce the essence of imperative, object-oriented, functional, logical, concurrent and distributed programming through a study of the Kernel Language together with well chosen laboratory programming problems and pre-programmed examples in Oz.

8.3 CS-2

Update the usual set of algorithms and data structures covered in conventional CS-1 and CS-2 and illustrate them with problems and pre-programmed examples. Show how to use Kernel Language programming and reasoning skills to rapidly acquire conventional language (e.g. Java) programming skills.

8.4 ProgLangs

Introduce students to different programming languages and paradigms via net-centric multi-language multi-platform programming using dotNET or a similar multi-language, multi-platform programming system.

9. INTRODUCTORY CURRICULUM FOR NINTENDO GENERATION STUDENTS

In the April 2002 issue of CACM, Mark Guzdial and Elliot Soloway [17] recognize that even in a down-turned economy many programming jobs go unfilled while the dropout/failure rate in CS-1 courses is in the 15% - 30% range. They quote a report [18] that found shockingly low performance on simple problems even among 2nd year college students, surveying 4 schools in 3 different countries.

Soloway & Guzdial note that engaging the students is critical to deep learning. They observe that "Hello World!" and other text-based programming problems do not engage today's students. They suggest that multimedia programming will most likely engage the full attention and energy of today's Nintendo, MTV generation of students.

9.1 CS-1

Introduce programming concepts through practical web-page construction in the laboratory. Explain each concept with the help of the Kernel Language in a "just-in-time" fashion.

9.2 CS-2

Introduce net-centric, multi-thread, multi-platform programming skills. Explain concepts with Kernel Language. Motivate the use of CS-1, CS-2 covered data structures and algorithms by suitably chosen laboratory excercises. Provide pre-programmed examples in Oz. Extend to multi-language programming along the lines of Bertrand Meyer's two-language Ticket Reservation System example [19].

9.3 ProgLangs

Use Kernel Language to teach what is common to all paradigms and how the paradigms differ. Teach how to use Kernel Language Knowledge to rapidly acquire programming skills in a widely used programming language e.g. Java.

10. THE DOTNET EFFECT

Mozart-Oz is a well-designed, well-implemented multi-paradigm, multi-thread and multi-platform programming system. At New Mexico State University, our experience with teaching programming with Mozart-Oz and the Kernel Language echoes the results reported by Van Roy [8]. Our students have also commented that they finally understood what the Java or C++ course had tried to teach them only after they were able to discuss these programming concepts in terms of the Kernel Language in our Mozart-Oz based programming course.

Before dotNET [20], one could ask whether our view of multi-paradigm programming might be too rosy, too optimistic. One could ask if multi-paradigm, multi-thread, multi-platform programming has a practical future.

Now that dotNET, initiated by Microsoft and supported by a consortium of major companies including IBM, Intel and HP, has shown that multi-language, net-centric, multi-platform programming is indeed possible and available, we urgently need a programmer's theory of programming with which to manage all this new knowledge that the next generation of programmers will need. One-language programming will be made obsoleteby dotNET and its successors. Therefore the sooner we can find new, more appropriate and effective ways to teach programming the better.

11. CONCLUSIONS

The Kernel Language approach provides a programmer's theory of programming, which programmers can use to reason about programs using terms and concepts that are already familiar to programmers.

The trend to multi-language, multi-paradigm, multi-thread, multi-platform programming that was initiated by dotNET, requires urgent redefinition of our one-language based CS-1, CS-2 introductory programming course sequence.

Another reason for urgent revision of the introductory programming course sequence is the student disenchantment with the text-based, "Hello World" type programming problems and program examples of current courses.

Therefore we should look very seriously and with some urgency at a redesign of the CS and Software Engineering introductory course sequence to make the courses more relevant for the programming requirements as well as the student expectations of tomorrow.

12. ACKNOWLEDGEMENTS

The author is grateful to Peter Van Roy for two immensely intensive days in December 1999 when Peter taught me the basics of Oz programming. The author is grateful to Seif Haridi for the opportunity to spend a week at the Swedish Institute for Computer Science to meet with experienced Mozart-Oz programmers, especially Fredrick Holmgren who showed me how to do agent based programming in Oz. The author acknowledges the Mozart Consortium for the design of the programming language Oz that makes programming a pleasure and for the Mozart system that implements Oz so effectively and reliably.

13. REFERENCES

[1]   Meyer, B., "The Power of a Unifying View", Software Development, June 2001.
[2]   ACM Curriculum Committee, "Curriculum 68", CACM Vol. 11, #3, p.151-197, (1968)
[3]   Sammet, J. E., "Programming Languages: History & Fundamentals", Prentice Hall (1969)
[4]   ACM Curriculum Committee, "Curriculum'78", CACM Vol. 22, #3, p.147-167, (1979)
[5]   Knox, D., (Ed.), "Proceedings of the 33rd SIGCSE Technical Symposium on Computer Science Education, Feb. 27 – March 3, 2002, North Kentucky, ACM Press (2002)
[6]   Tucker, A. B., Ed., "Computing Curricula 1991", http://www.acm.org/education/curr91/ homepage.html, IEEE Computer Society Press (1991)
[7]   Computing Curricula 2001, CS Volume 1, http://www.acm.org/sigcse/cc2001/
[8]   Van Roy, P., Haridi, S., "Teaching Programming Broadly and Deeply: the Kernel Language Approach", (this volume), Kluwer Academic Publishers (2002)
[9]   Dijkstra, E. W., "A Discipline of Programming", Prentice Hall (1976, 1997)
[10] Gries, D., "The Science of Programming", Springer (1981)
[11] van de Snepscheut, J. L. A., "What Computing is All About", Springer (1993)
[12] Mozart Consortium, http://www.mozart-oz.org
[13] Van Roy, P., Haridi, S., http://www.info.ucl.ac.be/people.PVR/book.html
[14] Wilson, L. B., Clark, R. G., "Comparative Programming Languages", Add. Wes. (1988)
[15] Reinfelds, J., "A Three Paradigm Course for CS Majors", Proceedings, 26th ACM SIGCSE Technical Symposium on Computer Science Education, p.223-227, (1995)
[16] Reinfelds, J., "1996 Lecture Notes for CS 272 (new)", 251 pages, Department of Computer Science, New Mexico State University (1996, 1997) .
[17] Guzdial, M., Soloway, E., "Teaching the Nintendo Generation to Program", CACM Vol. 45, #4, p.17-21, (2002).
[18] Mc Cracken, M., et al., "A multinational, multi-institutional study of assessment of programming skills of first-year CS students", ACM SIGCSE Bul. 33, 4, p.125-140 (2001)

[19] Meyer, B., "A multi-language example using Eiffel#, C# and ASP+ in dotNET", http://www.dotnet.eiffel.com, (2002).

[20] Meyer, B., "The Significance of dotNET", IEEE Computer, August 2001.

Teaching Programming Broadly and Deeply:
The Kernel Language Approach

Peter Van Roy
Department of Computing Science and Engineering (INGI)
Université catholique de Louvain (UCL)
B-1348 Louvain-la-Neuve Belgium
pvr@info.ucl.ac.be

Seif Haridi
Department of Microelectronics and Information Technology (IMIT)
Royal Institute of Technology (KTH)
S-164 28 Kista Sweden
seif@it.kth.se

Abstract: We present the *kernel language approach;* a new way to teach programming that situates most of the widely known programming paradigms (including imperative, object-oriented, concurrent, logic, and functional) into a uniform setting that shows their deep relationships and how to use them together. Widely different practical languages (exemplified by Java, Haskell, Prolog, and Erlang) with their rich panoplies of abstractions and syntax are explained by straightforward translations into closely related *kernel languages*, simple languages that consist of small numbers of *programmer-significant* concepts. Kernel languages are easy to understand and have a simple formal semantics that can be used by practicing programmers to reason about correctness and complexity.

Key words: computer programming, education, curriculum, science, engineering, programming concepts, programming paradigms, kernel language, dataflow, concurrency, functional programming, object-oriented programming, logic programming, imperative programming, programming techniques

1. EXISTING APPROACHES

For the purposes of this paper, let us consider a broad definition of computer programming as bridging the gap between the specification and the running program. This consists of designing the architecture and abstractions of an application and coding them in a programming language. Programming as a discipline has two essential parts: a technology and its scientific foundation. The technology consists of tools, practical techniques, and standards, allowing one to *do* programming. The science consists of a broad and deep theory with predictive power, allowing one to *understand* programming. The science should be designed to be useful to the practical programmer, to allow him or her to reason about correctness and complexity of practical programs.

Surprisingly, we find that programming is not taught in this way. Rather, it is taught in two different ways: either as a craft in the context of a single programming paradigm and its tools, or as a branch of mathematics. The science is either limited to the chosen paradigm or too fundamental to be of practical use. Let us survey the main focus of existing textbooks: object-oriented programming [15, 21, 24, 25,] imperative programming [22], functional programming [6, 10, 13, 18, 23], logic programming [7, 31], functional/imperative programming [1, 14, 16], and concurrent imperative programming [3, 4]. Some textbooks are explicitly limited to a particular language [4, 5, 7, 9, 20, 21 24, 25, 31, 32]. Almost no attempt is made to put the paradigms in a uniform framework. The only achievement is to show how object-oriented programming can be explained in terms of functional programming and state. A more explicit attempt is Leda [8], but it presents only a few paradigms and does not explain in any depth how to use them together or how they are related. None of these textbooks give a formal semantics except for those on functional programming and concurrent imperative programming. Specialized books on language semantics are either too formal or too restricted for the wider concerns of practical programming [12, 19, 27, 34].

Taken together, these textbooks show programming as a discipline lacking unity. This has a detrimental effect on programmer competence and thus on program quality. A concrete example illustrating this is concurrent programming in Java. Concurrency with shared state and monitors, as used in many languages including Java, is so complicated that it is taught only in advanced courses [20]. Furthermore, the implementation of concurrency in current versions of Java is expensive. Java-taught programmers reach the conclusion that concurrency is *always* complicated and expensive. They write programs to avoid concurrency, often in a contorted way. But these limitations are not fundamental at all; there are useful forms of concurrency, such as dataflow concurrency (e.g., streams in Unix) and active objects, which are almost as easy to use as sequential programming. Furthermore, it is possible to implement threads almost as cheaply as procedure calls. Teaching concurrency in a broader way would allow programmers to design and program with concurrency in systems without these limitations, including improved implementations of Java.

2. THE KERNEL LANGUAGE APPROACH

How can we teach students the broad view? There are simply too many programming languages to teach them all. Teaching a few carefully selected languages, say one per paradigm (for example Java, Prolog, and Haskell), is a stopgap solution. It multiplies the intellectual effort of the student (since each language has its own syntax and semantics) and does not show the deep connections between the paradigms. The kernel language approach we propose solves these problems.

The approach is not based on a single language (or a few languages), but on the underlying concepts. The concepts are carefully chosen to be meaningful for practical programming. They are organized into simple languages called *kernel languages*. Practical languages in all their richness are translated into the kernel languages in a straightforward manner. This approach is truly language-independent; a wide variety of languages and programming paradigms can be modelled by a small set of closely related kernel languages.

The kernel languages are easy to understand and have a simple formal semantics that allows practicing programmers to reason about correctness and complexity at a high level of abstraction. Programming paradigms and their requisite languages are then emergent phenomena, depending on which concepts one uses. The advantages and limitations of each paradigm show up clearly. This gives the student a deep and broad insight into programming concepts and how to use them to design abstractions. For example, many of our students who were already proficient Java programmers have told us that they first understood what Java objects really were after following our course.

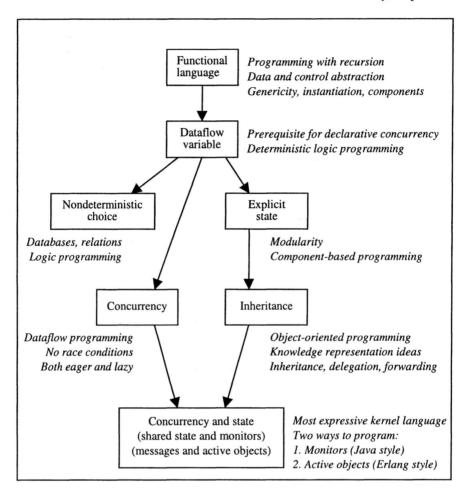

Figure 1. Some important steps in the kernel language approach.

Figure 1 briefly summarizes how we organize programming according to this approach. Each box corresponds to a kernel language. The figure is incomplete; our textbook distinguishes more than 20 paradigms, each with its kernel language. Here are some important steps:

–   The most basic kernel language does strict functional programming. This can already express most of the programming techniques of the later kernel languages. It can express data and control abstraction, genericity, instantiation, and components.

–   The second kernel language adds dataflow variables (a kind of single-assignment variable). This is essential for two reasons. It is a prerequisite for declarative concurrency. It also means that the second language is a deterministic logic programming language.

- We add nondeterministic choice to the second language. This gives relational programming and nondeterministic logic programming.
- We add concurrency to the second language. This gives a form of dataflow programming that is both purely functional and concurrent. We call it declarative concurrency. It is as easy to reason in as sequential functional programming. Eager execution and lazy execution are the two complementary ways to use declarative concurrency.
- We add explicit state to the second language. State is essential for modularity, because it allows changing a component's behavior over time without changing its interface. Object-oriented programming is a way of programming with state that adds concepts from knowledge representation, such as subtyping, class hierarchies, and associations. This leads to new program structuring techniques such as inheritance, delegation, and forwarding. All the techniques of the first language can be transferred to object-oriented programming.
- Using both concurrency and state together gives a language that is very expressive but also hard to program and reason in. There are two main approaches to master its complexity: using coarse-grained atomic actions such as monitors, or using message passing between active objects.

Within these languages and others, we discuss different forms of abstraction, nondeterminism, encapsulation, compositionality, security, and other important concepts. We give a simple operational semantics for all kernel languages. We show how some of the kernel languages can use other semantics such as axiomatic and logical semantics.

The kernel language approach is an outgrowth of ten years of programming language research and implementation by an international team, the Mozart Consortium, which consists of the Swedish Institute of Computer Science and the Royal Institute of Technology (KTH) in Sweden, the Universität des Saarlandes in Germany, and the Université Catholique de Louvain (UCL) in Belgium.

3. TEACHING EXPERIENCE

We first explain how we have realized the kernel language approach and our teaching experience with it. Based on this experience, we give recommendations on how to use the approach in an informatics curriculum.

3.1 Realization

We are writing a textbook *Concepts, Techniques, and Models of Computer Programming*. The latest draft is always available at:

http://www.info.ucl.ac.be/people/PVR/book.html

This draft is updated frequently and currently has more than 800 pages of material. It is intended for different levels of sophistication, ranging from second-year undergraduate courses to graduate courses. It assumes a previous exposure to programming and knowledge of simple mathematical concepts such as sequences and graphs. We have also prepared slides and lab sessions.

The textbook is supported by the Mozart Programming System, a full-featured open-source development platform that can run all program fragments in the book [26]. Full information including sources and binaries is available at the Mozart Web site:

http://www.mozart-oz.org

Mozart was originally developed as a vehicle for research in language design and implementation. We chose Mozart for the textbook because it implements the Oz language, which supports the kernel language approach perfectly well. Other reasons for picking Mozart are its implementation quality and its support for both Unix and Windows platforms.

The textbook mentions many languages and gives an in-depth treatment of four languages that are representative of widely different paradigms, namely Erlang, Haskell, Java, and Prolog. In a few pages it gives the essentials of each with respect to the kernel language approach and it gives the formal semantics of particularly interesting features.

3.2 Courses taught

The book draft and accompanying materials were used so far at three universities for the following courses:
- *DatalogiII 2G1512* (*Computer science II*, Fall 2001, 90 students, instructor Seif Haridi). Royal Institute of Technology (KTH), Kista, Sweden. For second-year students including both CS majors and non CS majors.
- *INGI2650* (*Structure of algorithmic programming languages*, Fall 2001, 55 students, instructor Peter Van Roy). Université catholique de Louvain (UCL), Louvain-la-Neuve, Belgium. For third-year CS students.

- *LINF1251* (*Introduction to programming part 2*, Spring 2002, 27 students, instructor Peter Van Roy). UCL. For second-year CS students. This follows a first-year introductory course based on a subset of Java.
- *INGI2655* (*Syntax and semantics of programming languages*, Spring 2002, 44 students, instructor Peter Van Roy). UCL. For fourth-year CS students. The book's operational semantics was used as a realistic example.
- *2G1915* (*Concurrent programming*, Spring 2002, 70 students, instructor Vladimir Vlassov). KTH. For fourth-year CS students. The chapter on concurrency and state was used.
- *EE 490/590* (Electrical and Computer Engineering Special Topics, instructor Juris Reinfelds). New Mexico State University, Las Cruces, New Mexico. Two CS graduate courses: *Distributed computing* (Fall 2001, 4 students) and *A programmer's theory of programming* (Spring 2002, 5 students). These courses and their motivation are covered in [30].

DatalogiII and INGI2650 were taught concurrently; they were the first time that the book was used for teaching. LINF1251 was the second time. Just for information, 64% passed DatalogiII,[1] 85% passed INGI2650, and 96% passed LINF1251. DatalogiII tried to teach too much material and the students (non CS majors) were less motivated. LINF1251 was more pedagogical: we adjusted the pace and all lectures were accompanied with live demonstrations and student interaction.

3.3 Curriculum recommendations

We have discussed the effects of the kernel language approach on the informatics curriculum with our colleagues at UCL, at workshops and conferences where we presented the approach, notably WCCE 2001 [2], MPOOL 2001 [11], and WFLP 2001 [17], and with other universities (notably the Katholieke Universiteit Leuven in Louvain, Belgium). Based on these discussions, we propose the following natural division of the discipline of programming into three core topics:
  1. Concepts and techniques.
  2. Algorithms and data structures.
  3. Program design and software engineering.
These topics are focused on the discipline of programming, independent of any other domain in informatics. Our textbook gives a thorough treatment of topic (1) and an introduction to (2) and (3). Parnas presents an approach that focuses on topic (3) [28] After discussion, we agree that a good approach is

---

[1] This percentage does not count students who will retake the exam in the future.

to teach (1) and (3) at the same time, introducing concepts and design principles concurrently [29]. In the informatics curriculum at UCL, we attribute eight semester-hours to each topic. This includes both lectures and lab sessions. Together the three topics comprise one sixth of the complete informatics curriculum.

4. CONCLUSIONS AND FURTHER READING

We have given a brief overview and motivation of the kernel language approach to teaching programming. The approach focuses on programming concepts and the techniques to use them ("concepts first"), not on programming languages or paradigms. Practical languages are translated into closely related kernel languages, simple languages that present the essential concepts in an intuitive and precise way. This gives students a view that is both broad and deep. The approach covers many programming paradigms and shows their deep relationships. It has a simple formal semantics that is usable by practicing programmers.

For further reading there is an extensive overview talk that introduces the kernel languages and their semantics and gives two highlights, in concurrent programming and graphic user interface programming [33]. We also recommend reading the Preface and Appendix E (General Computation Model) of the draft textbook.

5. ACKNOWLEDGMENTS

We thank our teaching assistants Raphaël Collet, Frej Drejhammer, Sameh El-Ansary, and Dragan Havelka. We also thank Juris Reinfelds, Dave Parnas, Elie Milgrom, and Yves Willems. Finally, we thank the members of the Mozart Consortium. This research is partly financed by the Walloon Region of Belgium in the PIRATES project and the Belgian Fonds National de la Recherche Scientifique (FNRS).

6. REFERENCES

[1] Abelson, H., Sussman, G. J., and Sussman, J. (1996). *Structure and Interpretation of Computer Programs, Second Edition*. The MIT Press.
[2] Andersen, J. and Mohr, C., editors (2001). *Seventh IFIP World Conference on Computers in Education*. UNI-C Denmark.
[3] Andrews, G. R. (1991). Concurrent Programming: Principles and Practice. Addison-Wesley.

[4] Armstrong, J., Williams, M., Wikström, C., and Virding, R. (1996). Concurrent Programming in Erlang. Prentice Hall.

[5] Arnold, K. and Gosling, J. (1998). The Java Programming Language, Second Edition. Addison-Wesley.

[6] Bird, R. (1998). Introduction to Functional Programming using Haskell, Second Edition. Prentice Hall.

[7] Bratko, I. (2001). Prolog Programming for Artificial Intelligence, Third Edition. Addison-Wesley.

[8] Budd, T. (1995). Multiparadigm Programming in Leda. Addison-Wesley.

[9] Chailloux, E., Manoury, P., and Pagano, B. (2000). Développement d'Applications avec Objective Caml. O'Reilly, Paris, France.

[10] Cousineau, G. and Mauny, M. (1998). The Functional Approach to Programming. Cambridge University Press.

[11] Davis, K., Smaragdakis, Y., and Striegnitz, J., editors (2001). Workshop on Multiparadigm Programming with Object-Oriented Languages (at ECOOP 2001), volume 7. John von Neumann Institute for Computing.

[12] Dijkstra, E. W. (1997). A Discipline of Programming. Prentice Hall. Original publication in 1976.

[13] Felleisen, M., Findler, R. B., Flatt, M., and Krishnamurthi, S. (2001). How to Design Programs: An Introduction to Computing and Programming. The MIT Press.

[14] Friedman, D. P., Wand, M., and Haynes, C. T. (1992). Essentials of Programming Languages. The MIT Press.

[15] Gamma, E., Helm, R., Johnson, R., Vlissides, J. (1994). Design Patterns: Elements of Reusable Object-Oriented Software. Addison-Wesley.

[16] Hailperin, M., Kaiser, B., and Knight, K. (1999). Concrete Abstractions: An Introduction to Computer Science Using Scheme. Brooks/Cole Publishing Company.

[17] Hanus, M., editor (2001). International Workshop on Functional and (Constraint) Logic Programming. Christian-Albrechts-Universität Kiel. Bericht Nr. 2017.

[18] Hudak, P. (2000). The Haskell School of Expression: Learning Functional Programming Through Multimedia. Cambridge University Press.

[19] Kirkerud, B. (1997). Programming Language Semantics: Imperative and Object Oriented Languages. International Thomson Computer Press.

[20] Lea, D. (2000). Concurrent Programming in Java, Second Edition. Addison-Wesley.

[21] Liskov, B. and Guttag, J. (2000). Program Development in Java: Abstraction, Specification, and Object-Oriented Design. Addison-Wesley.

[22] MacLennan, B. J. (1987). Principles of Programming Languages, Second Edition. Saunders, Harcourt Brace Jovanovich.

[23] MacLennan, B. J. (1990). Functional Programming: Practice and Theory. Addison-Wesley.

[24] Main, M. (1999). Data Structures & Other Objects using Java. Addison-Wesley.

[25] Meyer, B. (2000). Object-Oriented Software Construction, Second Edition. Prentice Hall.

[26] Mozart Consortium (2001). The Mozart Programming System, Version 1.2.3. See http://www.mozart-oz.org.

[27] Nielson, H. R. and Nielson, F. (1992). Semantics with Applications: A Formal Introduction. John Wiley & Sons.

[28] Parnas, D. (1995). Teaching Programming as Engineering. Ninth International Conference of Z Users (Springer LNCS 967). Reprinted in Software Fundamentals, Addison-Wesley, 2001.

[29] Parnas, D. (2002). Private communication.

[30] Reinfelds, J. (2002). Teaching of Programming with a Programmer's Theory of Programming. ICTEM 2002, Kluwer Academic Publishers.

[31] Sterling, L. and Shapiro, E. (1994). The Art of Prolog: Advanced Programming Techniques, Second Edition. Series in Logic Programming. The MIT Press.

[32] Stroustrup, B. (1997). The C++ Programming Language, Third Edition. Addison-Wesley.

[33] Van Roy, P. and Haridi, S. (2002). Teaching Programming both Broadly and Deeply: The Kernel Language Approach. Talks. See http://www.info.ucl.ac.be/people/PVR/book.html.

[34] Winskel, G. (1993). The Formal Semantics of Programming Languages. Foundations of Computing Series. The MIT Press.

Programming Strategies Using an Actor-Based Environment

Raul Sidnei Wazlawick and Antonio Carlos Mariani
UFSC-CTC-INE
Florianópolis, SC - Brazil
{raul,mariani}@inf.ufsc.br

Abstract   This text describes some programming strategies that computer science students have used to conduct programming tasks with an actor/stage metaphor. The authors maintain that the actor/stage metaphor is a useful strategy for teaching programming skills in the early classes of a computer science or engineering program, especially if a concurrent teaching strategy is used. The evidence of the success of this approach is that students in the first semester of a computer science course were able to develop many kinds of simulation software and games. This article shows some strategies that students have used, and the underlying concepts behind their approaches, and discusses the utility of the actor/stage metaphor as an educational tool.

1. INTRODUCTION

Programming languages are usually taught in computer science and engineering courses through a very strict bottom-up and sequential approach. However, Bertrand Meyer [1] has proposed to invert the Computer Science curriculum. However, any such attempt must rely on good methodologies and must be supported by high quality tools. Silveira and Scavarda-do-Carmo [2] have also discussed different techniques for teaching engineering, and proposed a mix of sequential and concurrent teaching, based on active learning and learning-by-doing for teaching engineering.

This paper describes some results of a five-year experience where a new approach to teaching programming has been tested. The methodology consists in asking first-year students to produce solutions to problems that seem complex for beginners, but that can be solved if a suitable metaphor is adopted.

It was found that the projects produced by students who use an actor/stage metaphor are far more complex and well structured than projects produced by students submitted to traditional teaching approaches.

2. BACKGROUND AND RELATED WORK

The tool "Actors' World", developed to support this kind of teaching method, was inspired initially by the Logo language and environment developed in the 1960's [3]. A second source of inspiration was Swarm [4], a software package for multi-agent simulation of complex systems. The main characteristic of Swarm that was incorporated by Actors' World was the implementation of an open architecture where different execution models could be implemented. The current version implements only the discrete events model, which is similar to that used in Swarm to describe agents' behavior. The main difference is in the notation used to describe behavior, which is similar in some aspects to that used in the Ágora environment [5].

The word "actor" in this environment is not intended to be consistent with that proposed by researchers such as Agha [6]. The concepts of stage and actors were chosen only to offer a metaphor to a clear and consistent interpretation in the world.

3. BASIC CONCEPTS

The programming tool Actors' World was developed in 1996 using the Smalltalk/V environment. It incorporates two major concepts: Actor and Stage.

Actors are instances of the Actor class. Actors behave like the turtle in the Logo language in the sense that they have a graphic representation, a position on the stage and a heading direction. Actors can move forward (method "go:") and turn around (method "turn:"). Actors can also sense if other actors are touching them, if a different actor is in the vicinity and so on. Each actor has a role that is specified by a set of sentences in the method "defineRole". Five basic kinds of sentences are allowed:

a) Unconditional action: defined by the method "alwaysDo:". For example,

```
self alwaysDo: [self go: 5; turn: 3]
```

b) Conditional action: defined by the method "when:do:". For example,
   `self when: [self isBeingTouched] do: [self go: 10]`
c) Fixed-interval actions: defined by the method "each:do:". For example,
   `self each: 30 do: [self go: 10]`
d) Probabilistic actions: defined by the method "withProbabilityOf:do:". For
   example: `self withProbabilityOf: 0.1 do: [self turn: 30]`
e) Specific time actions: defined by the method "at:do:". For example:
   `self at: 1000 do: [self leaveStage]`

The stage is the environment where actors live and interact. Each actor keeps a reference to the stage in which it is included, and the stage knows which actors it contains. The stage also controls the execution of the actors' roles, using a mechanism known as discrete events parallelism. Discrete events parallelism permits each actor to execute every unconditional sentence and every other kind of sentence that is supposed to be executed at that discrete instant of time without interruption. This is not real parallelism because there is not a real time-slice for each object. Using this approach, many problems related to object concurrency do not appear. For instance, debugging is still possible in Smalltalk, because sentences are executed orderly in discrete time. People trying to debug a real parallel Smalltalk program usually have a difficult time. One disadvantage of discrete event parallelism is that one single object can take over the processor by entering into a loop, and disabling other objects from running. But if a programming style with simple sentences is used instead of long and complex ones, then these problems usually do not occur.

4. STUDENTS' STRATEGIES IN ACTOR BASED PROGRAMMING

The course of object-oriented programming in the first year of the Computer Science career is based on a methodology similar to that proposed by Silveira and Scavarda-do-Carmo [2], where concepts are not viewed from bottom-up, but in parallel, and in a problem-driven way. Basic programming tools are presented to the students, who are then asked to develop applications. After working on some collective projects such as a traffic light system [7], they are asked to propose new projects. The teacher has to evaluate if the proposed projects are suitable in size and complexity for the student to be exposed to the main concepts of object oriented programming.

One group decided to implement a game based on "Space Invaders". The game has a mother ship that launches smaller ships. Each smaller ship launches bombs that fall to the ground, where a gun controlled by the user is located. The user is able to move the gun left and right, and fire missiles. A single missile can destroy a bomb or a small ship, but a lot of missiles are necessary to destroy the mother ship. It is evident that developing such a game is quite a challenge for a first year student, but using the expressive power of the actor based environment allowed this challenge to be accomplished relatively easily.

The solution involved the creation of the following actor classes: Gun, ExplodedGun, MotherShip, ExplodedMotherShip, Missile, Bomb, ExplodedBomb, ExplodedMissile, Ship, and ExplodedShip. The occurrence of these objects as graphic entities in the proposed problem helped the students to identify them correctly. Different behaviors between missile and exploded missiles, for example, were used to identify subclasses.

The Gun class has the following behavior: when it is off the stage, it comes back to the stage (the user cannot place the gun outside the stage), and when it is touched by an instance of an ExplodedBomb or an ExplodedShip, it becomes an ExplodedGun:

```
defineRole "in class Gun"
self when: [self outOfStage ] do: [self turn: 180; go: 35].
self when: [self touchesActorOfType: ExplodedBomb] do: [self
become: ExplodedGun].
self when: [self touchesActorOfType: ExplodedShip] do: [self
become: ExplodedGun].
```

An ExplodedGun and its counterparts have very simple behavior. Once created they have to exist for a short time and then disappear:

```
defineRole "in class ExplodedGun"
self at: 10 do: [self leaveStage].
```

Soon the student realizes that exploded things always have the same behavior, and that the existence of different classes of exploded things is not necessary, because the only difference is their image (bitmap) shown on the screen. At this point, it is a good idea to discuss the question of when it is interesting to have different subclasses or only a single class with different attributes.

The MotherShip behaves erratically. From time to time it jumps to a different region of the stage. Also, from time to time it launches a ship. When it touches any object it decreases its shields. When shields reach the value 0 it becomes an ExplodedMotherShip:

```
defineRole "in class MotherShip"
self each: 40 do: [self jump]. "jump is implemented elsewhere"
self each: 15 do: [self launchShip]. "launchShip if defined
below"
self when: [self touchAnActor] do: [live := live - 1].
self when: [live = 0] do: [self become: ExplodedMotherShip].
```

This kind of situation is useful for introducing the concept of instance variable. Also, method decomposition is explored at this stage because the student sees that it is simpler to read a method when it is decomposed in meaningful parts. The implementation of the method "launchShip" is:

```
launchShip "in class MotherShip"
| ship |
ship := Ship new.
ship enterStage: self stage. "the ship enters the same stage
as its mother ship"
ship jumpTo: self position. "the ship goes to the position of
the mother ship"
```

The definition of the other classes follows more or less the same pattern. A ship still has interesting behavior. It has to move around the stage, drop bombs, feel if it has touched the ground or an exploded missile and in this case becomes an ExplodedShip:

```
defineRole "in class Ship"
self alwaysDo: [self go: 4].
self withProbabilityOf: 0.2 do: [self dropBomb].
"the implementation of dropBomb is very similar to launchShip"
self when: [self hitGround] do: [self become: ExplodedShip].
"hitGround is simply a position test"
self when: [self touchActorOfType: ExplodedMissile] do: [self
become: ExplodedShip].
```

This project was successful and the final result was a fully playable game.

5. CONCLUSIONS

This experience has been remarkably surprising and gratifying. After using this approach with more than 300 students it was evident in each project developed that the underlying concepts of object-oriented programming were adequately learned from scratch, or reorganized when students already had misconceptions about object-oriented programming. Students proved that they were able to understand the concepts of object-oriented programming through this actor-based extension, and even when they implement their first system incorrectly, they were able to see better approaches. Some major difficulties with the syntax of the Smalltalk language are addressed in [7].

This approach to teaching programming is not limited to one semester. The method suggested is to start the course (first semester) with this actor-based extension to Smalltalk, so that students may learn the major concepts of object-oriented software analysis and synthesis. In the second semester it is suggested that students work with a typed language such as Eiffel, where types, exception handling, programming by contract, multiple inheritance and other concepts may be presented tó students that already have an idea of how to model a system. In the third semester it is suggested that students work with a medium level language, such as C++, where a traditional algorithmic approach may be presented. This third semester discipline may be combined with a course on data structures, where the student is supposed to develop classic algorithmic thinking.

As a continuation of this work a set of design patterns for student constructions in the Actors' World is under development. The catalog of design patterns is intended to help students in the future learn how to solve common programming tasks using this tool. Examples of common patterns are actors that reproduce themselves or that produce actors of different types, actors that react to touch, actors that react to the presence of other actors within a given range, and so on.

6. REFERENCES

[1] B. Meyer "Towards an Object-Oriented Curriculum" Symposium on Teaching Object Technology at TOOLS 11 (Technology of Object-Oriented Languages and Systems), Santa Barbara, August 1993; Prentice Hall, 1993, pages 585-594.

[2] M. A. da Silveira and L. C. Scavarda-do-Carmo, "Sequential and Concurrent Teaching: Structuring Hands-On Methodology", IEEE Transactions on Education, Vol. 42, No. 2, May 1999.

[3] S. Papert, "Mindstorms: Children, Computers and Powerful Ideas," New York. Basic Books, 1980.

[4] N. Minar, R. Burkhart, C. Langton, M. Askenazi, "The Swarm Simulation System: A Toolkit for Building Multi-agent Simulations," Santa Fe Institute, http://www.santafe.edu/projects/swarm/overview/overview.html, 1998.

[5] M. Q. Marchini and L. F. B. Melgarejo, "Ágora: Groupware Metaphors in Object-Oriented Concurrent Programming," in ECOOP 94 Workshop on Models and Languages for Coordination of Parallelism and Distribution, 1994.

[6] G. A. Agha, Actors: A Model of Concurrent Computation in Distributed Systems. Cambridge: MIT Press, 1986.

[7] R. S. Wazlawick and A. C. Mariani, "The Use of an Actor and Stage Metaphor for Introducing Object-Oriented Programming," IFIP World Computer Congress, 2000.

A Computing Program for Scientists and Engineers – What is the Core Of Computing?

Ralf Denzer
Environmental Informatics Institute; P.O. Box 11 12, 69251 Gaiberg, Germany;
Ralf.Denzer@enviromatics.org

Abstract   The education of non computer scientists in Information Technology basics becomes more important every day. We currently see a number of related effects in the educational and job market that force us to think about the requirements of minimal IT education for an engineer or a scientist. This paper, through a case study, raises questions related to these issues. The case study is a Curriculum on Environmental Informatics, which has been developed by the author and others under a grant by the European Union and the Canadian government. From this example, the paper tries to discuss the most important common roots in IT for engineers and scientists under heavy time constraints in their IT education. It will also reflect back on what this means for "pure" computer scientists.

Keywords: Computer Science Curricula, Enviromatics, EU Canada Program in Higher Education and Training

1. COMPUTING CURRICULA FOR COMPUTER SCIENTISTS AND NON COMPUTER SCIENTISTS

Computing curricula come in very different flavours across the world of higher education. Depending on the actual focus of an individual program, they are called *Computer Science* (CS), *Information Technology* (IT), *Information Science* (IS), Scientific *Computing* (SC), only to mention some of them. Although these terms are not clearly defined, and are often used differently and contradictorily in different countries, they usually imply a certain common understanding of the particular focus of the program. An example is the common understanding that CS is usually a "hard" scientific program based on a detailed discussion of computer science theory, while IS is a more "soft" program with different scientific standards. All these programs are needed for different areas of computing applications and different types of personnel in the job market and in the scientific community. *A Common Basis for Programs in Computing* would hence discuss those aspects of these programs that are the common core of these different programs in computing.

This paper has a different scope. The case study presented illustrates the needs of an IT education for *non IT professionals*, in particular for engineers and scientists, based on the experiences of more than 5 years of international collaboration in a Curriculum on Environmental Informatics [1], or *Enviromatics* [2].

Although the focus of these discussions is not primarily on computer scientists, we are convinced that the results can feed back to the "pure" computer science curricula as well. We develop software for users and these users are often a neglected part of the system.

2. COMPUTING FOR NON COMPUTER SCIENTISTS

There are three main reasons why we need to deal with computing curricula content for non computer scientists today. First, there is no scientific or engineering education today that would not require a basic understanding of computing. Often scientists and engineers become second career software developers. Second, there are many tools (like RDBMS with graphical front ends) that make it (supposedly) easy to develop an information system. Without the background knowledge of software engineering, untrained users of such tools often do a lot of nonsense. Third, the interface between the computer scientist and a "pseudo-trained" end user, often overestimating his or her understanding, is an issue we have to deal with today.

The two main questions evolving from these issues, which we wish to discuss in this article, are the following: a) If we are going to do a limited computing training of scientists and engineers, in what should we train them?; and b) What is particularly useful in the training of non computer scientists and in the training of computer scientists in order to make their interface in real life better?

3. CASE STUDY: COMPUTING FOR ENVIRONMENTAL SCIENTISTS AND ENGINEERS

Environmental protection is now unthinkable without the use of information systems and software tools for complex decision making processes. Many national and international organizations have been and still are building databases of environmental measurements and decision support software, e.g. for environmental impact assessment. Starting in the mid-1980's, a new applied discipline in Computer Science - which we now call *Environmental Informatics* or *Enviromatics* - evolved very quickly. In IFIP, it is represented by WG 5.11 of TC 5 (see www.enviromatics.org).

Due to the complexity and wide ranging aspects of such systems, we are still heterogeneous in our teaching activities which can be thought of as a basis for Environmental Informatics education. The extreme broadness of the application area on the one hand side and the many possibilities of software support on the other side means that it is very difficult for anybody to teach an Environmental Informatics course alone today. Environmental Informatics involves environmental monitoring, remote sensing, compliance, supervision by government agencies and other authorities, environmental research, planning, lifecycle assessment, etc. to mention some of them. The software side draws on scientific databases, visualization, modelling and simulation, artificial intelligence techniques as well as information retrieval and delivery over networks like the Internet. Environmental data management and environmental information systems have to bridge gaps in time and space in data, information and knowledge. Elements of modelling, statistical computing, scientific database, visualization, environmental statistics (including risk assessment), uncertainty estimation and management, integration of heterogeneous and legacy systems and knowledge engineering all contribute to a better understanding of environmental problems.

From 1997 to 2000, a group of European and Canadian universities conducted a project named ECCEI (EU Canada Curriculum on Environmental Informatics), which was funded under the EU Canada Program on Higher Education and Training. The goal of this project was (in addition to student and faculty exchange) the development of a curriculum for environmental information and decision support systems. With the curriculum, we intended to address computer scientists and environmental scientists and engineers.

A major problem in organizing the material was the ordering of the course modules. We discussed whether it is appropriate to use a primary order derived from IT technologies or one from environmental topics, the application areas. We finally came up with a curriculum design that progresses from less complex to more complex tasks, i.e. that follows the direction of more high level, abstract information generated by the information system. Table 1 shows the content of the curriculum.

If you add up the necessary hours to get only an overview of every topic, you end up with 120 to 150 hours of instruction. Clearly, each of the topics can be a course by itself and in that case, the curriculum would result in an environmental information systems specialist. Realistically, we are unable to teach all the topics in one course, even if it was a very big one. As far as we know, there is no EIS program either (world wide), which would offer such a curriculum as a BA or MA.

Our approach to cope with this situation was a rather unconventional method of teaching the course. Between 1997 and 2000, we taught no fewer than nine short courses with students from Germany, Canada, Italy and France. These courses typically extend over one week, host between 20 and 40 students and 5 to 10 faculty, each of them a specialist in more than one of the curricula topics. Most of the courses were taught in a specific location in Austria, an alpine farm house in a Nature Park, which offered us the possibility to set up seminar and computer lab facilities, conduct practical case studies and collect a lot of area related data over the years. After the three years of government funding, we continued with a core group from Canada, Germany and France and could also involve new partners from Austria and the United States.

The course starts with the definition of several projects (e.g. planning of a ski resort, assessment of flood risks in the valley or a public visual information system), which are then conducted in interdisciplinary teams. Typically, each team consists at least of one member from each participating university and of a mix of computer science students and environmental students. Theoretical parts are taught "on the fly", e.g. if one or more projects end up in a situation in which they need more background on certain methods or tools. After five days, the result of each team is expected to be a study, a methodology or (in most cases) a piece of software.

Table 7. ECCEI Curriculum

PART I: WHY ENVIROMATICS ?

1. History of Enviromatics Developments
2. Application Areas
3. Introduction into the ECCEI Course
4. Introduction into the Common Example

PART II: ENVIROMATICS BASE METHODS

SECTION II.A Problem Definition and System Analysis
5. Problem Definition
6. System Analysis

SECTION II.B Data Management and Information Modelling
7. Environmental Data, Data Preparation and Acquisition
8. Monitoring
9. Environmental Databases and Environmental Information Systems (EIS)
10. Information Modelling
11. Meta Information in Environmental Databases

SECTION II.C Data Analysis
12. Environmental Statistics
13. Geographical Information Systems
14. Visualization

SECTION II.D Diagnosis and Interpretation
15. Environmental Risk and Impact Assessment
16. Environmental Models
17. Environmental Indicators
18. Diagnosis and Artificial Intelligence

SECTION II.E Decision Support
19. Target Groups for Decision Support
20. IT Techniques and Systems for Decision Support
21. Scenarios
22. Presentation in DSS

PART III: ENVIROMATICS INTEGRATION METHODS

SECTION III.F EIS Interoperability
23. Integration Problems
24. Environmental Data Standards
25. Building and Managing Environmental Data Networks

SECTION III.G Meta Information Systems
26. Properties of Meta Information
27. Environmental Data Catalogs
28. Environmental Catalogs on the World Wide Web
29. Multilingual Information Systems

SECTION III.H Open EIS Architectures
30. Properties of Open EIS Architectures
31. Review of Architectures
32. Generic EIS Infrastructures

4. EXPERIENCES, DISCUSSIONS AND CONCLUSIONS

From the results and the interaction of our numerous courses, we have drawn the following main conclusions:

1. The most important and most effective module we teach to non computer scientists is basic information system modelling. Once these students get a minimal understanding of consistency, redundancy and complexity in information systems, and why computer scientists must use structured methods in their design to deal with these issues, they have a completely different perspective of information technology.

2. The most important aspect to learn for the computer scientists is that there are unstructured fields of knowledge (like environmental sciences) that lack a lot of the logic they are taught. One professor created the analogy of showing them that "the world is not a square box".

3. The most important overall experience of the courses is the interaction between groups, the human aspect. In many computing programs, there is no interaction of the students with real world users at all. In our courses, we create a real life project environment, which the students never see in our universities.

Coming back to the two questions introduced in section 2: a) We are strongly convinced that a minimum IT curriculum for scientists and engineers must contain issues of sound software engineering, before anything else; b) The joint interactive training of both groups together is a most useful vehicle for their later professional life. Teaching non computer scientists basic understanding of information system modelling (like ERMs) helps in communication between the groups.

5. SHORT BIOGRAPHY OF THE AUTHOR

Dr. Ralf Denzer is a professor for computer science in Saarbrücken, Germany. His main research area is distributed and open systems. Together with his colleague, Reiner Güttler, he is the director of the Environmental Informatics Group (www.enviromatics.net), an institute which has been working on more than 70 environmental information system projects, with a focus on integration of distributed information systems. He is chairman of the international Environmental Informatics Institute (www.enviromatics.de) and chairman of IFIP Working Group 5.11, Computers and Environment (www.enviromatics.org). He is adjunct professor at the University of

Guelph, On, Canada and adjunct professor at James Madison University, Va, USA.

6. REFERENCES

[1] D. A. Swayne, R. Denzer, Teaching EIS Development – *The EU Canada Curriculum on Environmental Informatics*, Environmental Software Systems Vol. 3 (2000) – Environmental Information and Decision Support, pp. 152-156, Kluwer Academic Publishers

[2] R. Denzer, *Environmental Software Systems*, Encyclopedia of Computer Science and Technology, Vol. 40(25), pp. 51-61, Marcel Dekker Publishers, 1999

Patterns of Curriculum Design

Douglas Blank and Deepak Kumar
Department of Mathematics & Computer Science
Bryn Mawr College, Bryn Mawr, PA 19010 (USA)
Email: {dblank, dkumar}@brynmawr.edu

Abstract   We present a perspective on the design of a curriculum for a new computer science program at a women's liberal arts college. The design incorporates lessons learned at the college in its successful implementation of other academic programs, incorporation of best practices in curriculum design at other colleges, results from studies performed on various computer science programs, and a significant number of our own ideas. Several observations and design decisions are presented as curriculum design patterns. The goal of making the design patterns explicit is to encourage a discussion on curriculum design that goes beyond the identification of core knowledge areas and courses.

1. INTRODUCTION

In this paper, we present a perspective on the design of a curriculum for a new computer science program at Bryn Mawr College. Founded in 1885, Bryn Mawr College is well known for the excellence of its academic programs. Bryn Mawr combines a distinguished undergraduate college for about 1200 women with two nationally ranked, coeducational graduate schools (Arts and Sciences, and Social Work and Social research) with about 600 students. As a women's college, Bryn Mawr has a longstanding and intrinsic commitment to prepare individuals to succeed in professional fields in which they have been historically underrepresented. In 1999, the college decided to add computer science to the college's academic programs. We are currently engaged in the expansion and design of the program. The design of the curriculum is being carried out based on several considerations that are discussed in this paper. The design incorporates lessons learned at the college in its successful implementation of other academic programs, incorporation of best practices in curriculum design at other colleges, results from studies performed on various computer science programs, and a significant number of our own ideas.

2. CURRICULUM DESIGN PERSPECTIVES

Margolis & Fisher have reported, based on a 5-year study of gender issues in computer science at Carnegie Mellon University, that female disinterest in computer science is not genetic, nor accidental, nor inherent to the discipline of computer science. It is largely due to three factors: early childhood gender socialization (at home); a combination of adolescence, peer relationships, computer game design, and secondary school social pressures; and the fact that female orientation towards (and concerns about) computing are different from the design of most computer science curricula[1].

The last issue is of particular concern to us. Margolis & Fisher claim that universities have historically developed computer science courses with a male bias. Thus, even the introductory courses in computer science are built around "male preferences" focusing on the very technical aspects from the very beginning. Further, based on interviews of over 100 female college students, they concluded that the female expression of lack of interest in computer science is really based on a lack of confidence.

At Bryn Mawr, we are currently engaged in the design of a new curriculum for computer science. While there exist prescribed and authoritative guidelines for a curriculum in computer science (the Association for Computing Machinery has announced a new basis for computer science curricula [2]), we are going about the design of our curriculum in an extremely independent and deliberative manner. This is partly in resonance with the findings of Margolis and Fisher, and largely based on our own experiences and similar findings at Bryn Mawr and at other universities. In the design of our curriculum, we are taking the challenge of engagement for women in computer science as our primary concern. Several design considerations have gone into the creation of our computer science curriculum: the context of the program within a women's liberal arts college; the context of computer science courses within the program; the requirements for a major; the design of a minor in computer science; and the design of everyday examples and exercises in all courses in computer science.

First and foremost, it is important to establish a place for computer science in a liberal arts college. Many computer science programs now reside in the school of engineering. Therefore, the question naturally arises: *If computer science has become a discipline of engineering, why offer it at a liberal arts college?* Without going into a lengthy response to this question, we will simply summarize it here by pointing out that while there are aspects of computer science that lean towards engineering, there are significantly more aspects of computer science that intersect with the broader goals of the liberal arts. In universities where career preparation is the main emphasis, computer science finds itself in the engineering school. In liberal arts colleges, the emphasis of a computer science program is on gathering, evaluating and disseminating knowledge with foundations in the area of logic, mathematics, and the sciences. We believe that taking a broader perspective on the nature of the discipline (we have proclaimed it to be a core liberal art of the future) and constantly including implications of technology and its use in society as well as in other academic disciplines will help stir a wider interest in computer science among students.

The view of computer science as a liberal art also leads to a re-examining of course offerings, as well as the content of various courses offered in the computer science program. Additionally, it leads one to re-evaluate the set of courses that, for an individual student, define a major (or a minor) in computer science. It further impacts the design of exercises and examples that are used in individual courses. In the process of designing our new computer science program for Bryn Mawr College, we have deliberated about all these issues at length. Below, we present some pertinent observations and design decisions that have affected our deliberations. While some of the observations arise out of formal studies conducted elsewhere, some are based on our own experiences and experiences shared by the global community of computer science faculty. We are not presenting them as a prescription for the design of all computer science programs, rather to facilitate a discussion on the underlying issues and their implication for curriculum design.

3. CURRICULUM DESIGN PATTERNS

We are calling our collections of observations and decisions curriculum design patterns after the "design patterns movement" in objected-oriented software design [3], which is based on the idea of design patterns developed by the architect Christopher Alexander: "Each pattern describes a problem which occurs over and over again in our environment, and then describes the core of the solution to that problem, in such a way that you can use this solution a million times over, without ever doing it the same way twice." [4]

4. COMPUTING ACROSS THE CURRICULUM, NOT!

Our starting point is to defer from the obvious notion of "computing across the curriculum." Several disciplines have adopted such an approach: "writing across the curriculum" or, more recently, "mathematics across the curriculum." Given the pervasive nature of computing in these times, it would be an obvious choice to champion computing across the college as a way to engage women in computer science. However, we strongly feel that affecting another department or program's curriculum *is* an imposition and it is unclear whether it will result in more students engaged (or favorably disposed) into further study in computer science. While there have been documented successes of the *writing across the curriculum* and *mathematics across the curriculum* for non-English majors and non-mathematics majors, there is no evidence that such initiatives lead to more engagement in English and Mathematics majors.

For computer science to become a sought after and engaging field of study, we believe that it is our program's responsibility to demonstrate in effective ways how computing has become pervasive in today's society, and hence we have taken a fresh look at the context in which the program sits at a college like Bryn Mawr. From a curriculum design perspective, our response is to concentrate on courses within computer science. There are several courses that are explicitly created for *all* students at the college, and there are also upper-level computer science electives that are also open to non-computer science students. The objective of the design of these courses is to go well beyond the goal of achieving *fluency* to a more intellectual level discourse of ideas and concepts of which fluency may just be one of the *side effects*. This has resulted in several courses that are offered in the computer science program. These are presented in the next three sections.

5. PARTICIPATION IN THE FRESHMAN SEMINARS

All students entering Bryn Mawr College are required to take two freshman-level *college seminar* courses. These courses are designed as pre-disciplinary expositions that encourage critical thinking in addition to developing strong writing skills. In our computer science program, we have made the commitment to offer at least one course each year in the college seminar program. This has led to the design and creation of a diverse range of courses at a pre-disciplinary level with a basis in computer science and technology. The topic areas change from year to year. Here are two recent offerings:

Weaving the web: A course that examines the history of the development of the worldwide web, its current use, and its implications in the global society. Eighteen students enrolled constitute the editorial board of a web-based magazine. Students learn the technology underlying web design and *all* written work is in the form of articles for the web magazine. The scope of the magazine is to discuss issues relating to technology and its implications on the Bryn Mawr community [5].

Robots gone berserk--- A look at robots in film: A course that examines portrayals of robots in film and compares it to the state-of-the-art in Artificial Intelligence and Cognitive Science. Described to students as, "This College Seminar is not a writing course. It is not a film course. It is not a robotics course. It is not a science fiction course. Although, come to think of it, we will write some papers. We will watch some movies. We will study some robotics. And we will read some science fiction. However, this course is really about thinking. In fact, we will spend quite a bit of time thinking about thinking." [6]

6. A TERMINAL CS1 COURSE IS TERMINAL, FOR WOMEN

Most universities offer two versions of an introductory level course in computer science: One designed for students who wish to major in computer science; one designed for those who do not. Our claim is that most women who otherwise might go on to major in computer science, due to lack of confidence, self-select themselves into the *terminal* non-majors version of the course. This is a subtle observation that most formal studies about gender equity will tend to overlook and hence is unlikely to be uncovered in any study. At Bryn Mawr, we offer only one version of the introductory course. Traditionally, 3/4 of the students in this course are from non-science majors.

7. UPPER-LEVEL ELECTIVES ARE INTERDISCIPLINARY

In order to further the intellectual engagement of all Bryn Mawr students in computer science, several upper-level computer science courses are designed so that they are also accessible to students in other disciplines. The issue of non-majors not meeting a particular course's prerequisites is addressed by expanding the scope of the course by relating it to topics and disciplines outside of computer science, as well as by including team-oriented exercises where each team is comprised of students from diverse disciplines contributing and exchanging ideas and perspectives. Examples include the following courses:

Cognitive Science: Open to students in all disciplines. Also cross-listed in the philosophy department.

Artificial Intelligence: Open to students in all disciplines. Also cross-listed in the Philosophy department.

Digital Multimedia: Open to students of all disciplines (will be offered for the first time in Spring 2003).

Recent Advances in Computer Science: This is a special topics course. Enrollment is open, depending on the specific topic. Example topics: *Computer-related Risks:* Open to students in all disciplines. *Biologically Inspired Computational Models of learning:* Open to all science majors (as well as graduate students).

Thus, by reexamining the notion of *computing across the curriculum*, and beginning from within the computer science program, we have *opened up* access to the field of computer science to the wider community of students at Bryn Mawr College. This has affected the design of courses at the freshman/predisciplinary-level, introductory level, as well several upper-level electives.

8. HUMANIZING CORE COMPUTER SCIENCE COURSES

Within computer science, the design of each core course is an amalgamation of the concepts underlying the topic of the course (as recognized by the larger computer science community) and the social and cultural implications of the topic in society. For example, consider the course, *Principles of Programming Languages.* This is considered a core course in computer science. It is largely concerned with the principles underlying the design of programming languages. Traditionally flooded with technical content, the course has been redesigned to include case studies of practitioner's lives. There are several biographies and essays available that describe the lives of computer scientists who could be classified as "programming language experts" [7, 8, 9, 10]. Some of them have been designers of prominent programming languages, while some have led commercial ventures based on programming language products. Thus, a *human element* is included in the course without necessarily sacrificing the technical matter. Other so-called technical courses in computer science are also being designed in this manner.

9. DESIGN OF EVERYDAY LECTURE ARTEFACTS

In a liberal arts setting, the nature of examples and exercises used in day-to-day lectures also requires careful attention. Computer science, like most other disciplines in the sciences, has suffered from indulging its students in exercises and examples from within the discipline. In our view of computer science as a liberal art, where possible, we encourage the use of examples and exercises that are taken from diverse disciplines, especially focusing on non-science areas like archaeology, linguistics, economics, environmental studies, etc. We are currently in the process of designing a formal multi-year study fn the use of examples and assignments in computer science courses.

10. BREAKING RIGID BOUNDARIES

Often, a curriculum is packed tightly with a well thought out design of topics and their prerequisites. In addition, each course is packed tightly with materials related to a particular topic. We believe that it is more advantageous to cover less material in a particular topic in exchange for connecting the topic more thoroughly to other areas in, and out of, computer science. For example, consider a course on data structures. Normally, ideas such as parallelism would not (or could not) be mentioned in such a course. However, by breaking down the rigid, and often artificial, boundaries between topics, we believe that concepts learned by students will be more solid and well founded. This methodology does require faculty to communicate closely to ensure that no big ideas are missed. Faculty should also be encouraged to be extremely opportunistic about bringing ideas from their own research into the classroom.

11. CREATING ROOM IN THE CURRICULUM

We have observed that several middle to upper-level undergraduate computer science courses at larger universities (especially those with Masters and PhD programs) are often cross-registered into their graduate program's offerings. For example, in many universities, a single offering of courses on *theory of computation, operating systems, compiler construction*, etc. exists in which both graduate and undergraduate students enroll at the same time. This has led us to reexamine our own set of middle/upper-level course offerings. For courses that we feel are essential to the knowledge of an undergraduate computer science major, we have included them in our curriculum. We have eliminated most courses that are required to be taken by graduate students and are not necessarily considered essential for an undergraduate degree. This has two significant effects: first, it creates *room* in the curriculum for creating newer, more innovative courses; second, for the traditional courses that we do include, we design their curriculum tailored more towards an undergraduate level, as opposed to an offering that is also required to satisfy the knowledge requirements for a graduate-level course.

12. FLEXIBILITY IN DESIGNING A MAJOR

What set of courses constitutes a major in computer science? The Curriculum 2001 report outlines a *core* body of knowledge that every computer science major should learn [2]. The report recommends that the core be complemented with additional coursework in other areas of computer science. In our program, consistent with the college's requirements for a total of 12 courses to be taken in a major, the following program is recommended for a computer science major:

Introductory Courses: These include our own instantiations of CS1, CS2, and Discrete Mathematics.

Core Courses: Students are required to take a course on principles of computer organization, principles of programming languages, and one course in algorithm design and analysis.

Systems Courses: Students have to take a course in either compiler design or operating systems.

Electives: Five additional courses in computer science based on the student's choosing.

Senior Thesis: All computer science majors also complete a senior project/thesis.

These requirements provide tremendous flexibility to each student since they provide the freedom to choose nearly 50% of their required courses based on their own personal interests.

13. MINOR IN COMPUTER SCIENCE FOR ALL

Any student majoring in any discipline can do a minor in computer science at Bryn Mawr College. In most schools, the minor (or concentration) is typically an option available only to students majoring in mathematics and natural sciences. However, with the increasing pervasiveness of computing, we have felt it essential to open the entryways into computer science for all students. The requirements of a minor in computer science are:

Introductory Courses: These include our own instantiations of CS1, CS2, and Discrete Mathematics.

Core Courses: Any two of the core courses in computer science: Principles of Computer Organization, Principles of Programming Languages, Algorithms: Design & Practice, Analysis of Algorithms, and Theory of Computation.

Electives: Two additional courses in computer science based on the student's choosing.

14. MAJORS IN EMERGING COMPUTATIONAL DISCIPLINES

Our program also encourages interested students to design independent majors in emerging computational disciplines like cognitive science, computational chemistry, computational physics, bioinformatics, geoinformatics, computational linguistics, etc. Students consult with faculty advisors in designing their programs of study. The course selections are tailored to student interests. While the computer science program becomes a default home of such majors, significant participation is necessary from faculty in other disciplines as well. Our program has been successful in influencing faculty-hiring decisions in other programs to bring in faculty with interests overlapping with computer science. Occasionally, students will also take courses offered in other area institutions. We consider ourselves lucky to be situated in a region that has more than a dozen colleges and universities in the same metropolitan area.

15. SUMMARY

In this paper, we have presented several design considerations that form the basis of our evolving computer science program. As is evident, there is much more to curriculum design than instantiating a prescription of knowledge areas into various courses. The design patterns presented above are by no means exhaustive, nor even attempting to be complete or universal. While Christopher Alexander evolved the idea of patterns in the context of architectural design, and it was later applied to object-oriented design, it applies equally well in the context of curriculum design. It is also in this sense that the patterns presented in this paper are to be taken as points for further discussion, rather than as a prescription for all curricula.

16. REFERENCES

[1]   Margolis, Jane & Fisher, Allan, Unlocking the Clubhouse: Women in Computing. Cambridge, MA: MIT Press, 2002.
[2]   IEEE-CS & ACM, Computing Curricula 2001: Computer Science Volume, available on the worldwide web at: http://www.acm.org/sigcse/cc2001. IEEE-CS/ACM, 2001.
[3]   Gamma, E., Helm, R., Johnson, R., Vlissides, J., Design Patterns: Elements of Reusable Object-Oriented Software. Reading, MA: Addison-Wesley, 1994.
[4]   Alexander, C., Ishikawa, S., Silverstein, M., Jacobson, M., Fiksdahl-King, I., Angel, S., A Pattern Language. New York: Oxford University Press, 1977.
[5]   Bryn Mawr College Computer Science Program worldwide web page: http://cs.brynmawr.edu.
[6]   Robots gone berserk: A look at robots in film, Bryn Mawr College course web page: http://dangermouse.brynmawr.edu/csem.
[7]   Gabriel, Richard P., Patterns of Software: Tales from the software community. Oxford: Oxford University Press, 1996.
[8]   Shasha, D., Lazaere, C., Out of their minds: The lives and discoveries of 15 great computer scientists. New York: Copernicus, 1995.
[9]   Brooks, Rodney A., Flesh and machines: How robots will change us. New York: Pantheon Books, 2002.
[10] Dijkstra, Edsger W., Selected writings on computing: A personal perspective. New York: Springer-Verlag, 1982.

Variations in Computing Science's Disciplinary Diversity [2]
The case of curricula recommendations

Luiz Ernesto Merkle
Centro Federal de Educação Tecnológica do Paraná - Departamento Acadêmico de Informática - Av. Sete de Setembro, 3165 - Centro, Curitiba, PR, Brazil, 80230-901 merkle@ppgte.cefetpr.br

Robert E. Mercer
The University of Western Ontario -- Department of Computer Science, MC 355   London, Ontario, Canada, N6A 5B7 mercer@csd.uow.ca

Abstract: This article graphically explores the historical development of Informatics using the trajectory of curricula recommendations in Computing Science. Faced with the disciplinary diversity found in ACM computing curricula recommendations and related documents, the usual description of Informatics as an ever expanding field is challenged. Indeed, in the first period the disciplinary diversity fostered by the community was reduced. This reduction of diversity was accompanied by an increase in the depth of a few branches, structuring Informatics in areas such as Computer Engineering, Computing Science, and Information Systems. Since then, Informatics' footprint has increased, demanding a renewal of its disciplinary structure, which triggered the emergence of new related occupations. The graphic representations proposed here motivate a discussion of current professional tendencies, illustrating that Informatics history is richer than it is usually seen.

Key words: Computers and Education, History of Informatics, Disciplinary Diversity, Curricula Recommendations

1. INTRODUCTION

A set of disciplinary events and transformations has taken place across Informatics' lifespan. As Informatics' areas of expertise developed and its

[2] This article is partially based on Merkle [7, Chapter 1].

niches were explored, they not only matured, but also established a corresponding division of labour. Throughout the process, unexplored gaps, abandoned niches, and reinforced barriers enabled the emergence, the maintenance, and the decay of disciplinary practices, old and new. It is usual to describe Informatics' related disciplines, such as the ones focusing on computing and information systems, as being in a rapid and constant expansion, as having an identity grounded on constant innovation, and as being the foundations for an envisioned social revolution.

Nevertheless, it has not been critically questioned how the disciplinary profile fostered throughout its development has varied; at least by most of those who work in Informatics. It is unquestionable that Informatics' consolidation can be associated with the great depth that its communities have developed within certain subjects. In terms of disciplinary breadth, however, over-specialization is a drawback, considering the demand for professionals who can work and communicate effectively.

Indeed, the widespread assumption that Informatics is an ever-expanding field does not correspond to the actual disciplinary variations found across its historical development. During Informatics' inception phase (until the 1960s), it had a higher disciplinary diversity than it was able to maintain during the seventies and eighties. During that first period, areas such as Anthropology, Linguistics, Design, Human Factors, Psychology, Industrial Engineering, and others were mentioned as contributing to the field. From that initial diversity, only some branches have been consolidated within the community, in fields such as Computer Engineering, Computing Science, and Information Systems. The rest became dormant, remained on the outskirts of particular disciplinary branches, or developed elsewhere. Information Science is an example of the latter.

Throughout this historical process of consolidation, the involved communities raised many barriers and bridges that ended up structuring Informatics as it is known today. Computer Engineering, Computing Science and Information Systems developed narrow but complementary constellations of interests focused on hardware, software, and systems, respectively. Interests in cybernetics, systemic approaches, linguistics, and anthropology have been slowly left out of the core issues of the profession. This decrease in diversity and increase in focus may have been appropriate in the past, but it is under revision now. Awareness of these dynamics can help the reorganization of Informatics as a whole, including a better understanding and appraisal of the roles that some recently emerged fields can play.

As traditional disciplinary branches became too insular, or as the cultural role of Informatics in society grew beyond its niche of expertise, theories and practices started to become insufficient to account for the richness of its consequences. Given the opportunity, other branches emerged, such as Software Engineering and Human-Computer Interaction, increasing the established disciplinary diversity. Currently, the field is in a transition period and no disciplinary dynamics have stabilized yet. The introduced novelty has been challenging professionals, educators, law and policy makers, and politicians, who have neither grounds nor background to decide in which direction to go, or in what or whom to invest.

2. HISTORICAL DEVELOPMENT OF INFORMATICS

Figure 1 gives a synoptic view of the curricula recommendations and related documents published mainly in the United States. The graphic organization of the diagram is in accordance with the Unified Classification Scheme for Informatics, developed by Mulder and van Weert [8], cited in Mulder and van Weert [9, pp109-111], but it was not based on it.

It took a long time for Informatics to be recognized in the academic milieu. Although the criticisms were many, it continued to develop. As it developed, their social implications and consequences increased, but the disciplinary diversity of Informatics as a whole decreased. In terms of disciplinary relations, the consolidation of a field is concomitant with the construction of its identity and subject matter. Therefore, there is a tendency to narrow the kind of phenomena that a field encompasses during its inception.

For example, in 1954, a few years after the Association for Computing Machinery (ACM) was founded, its president, Samuel B. Williams, explained that the ACM was going to focus on what later became known as software and systems and their use, withdrawing hardware to engineering [14, p3]. This illustrates a historical watershed between two periods: a first period in which the American Institute of Electrical Engineers, the Institute of Radio Engineers, and the then recently formed Association for Computing Machinery were organizing joint conferences, for example; and a second period in which the communities started to narrow down their interests in order to deepen their foundations. Through this process, the fields of Computer Engineering, Computing Science, and Information Systems slowly emerged, and became recognized across academia, industry, commerce, government, and other cultural venues.

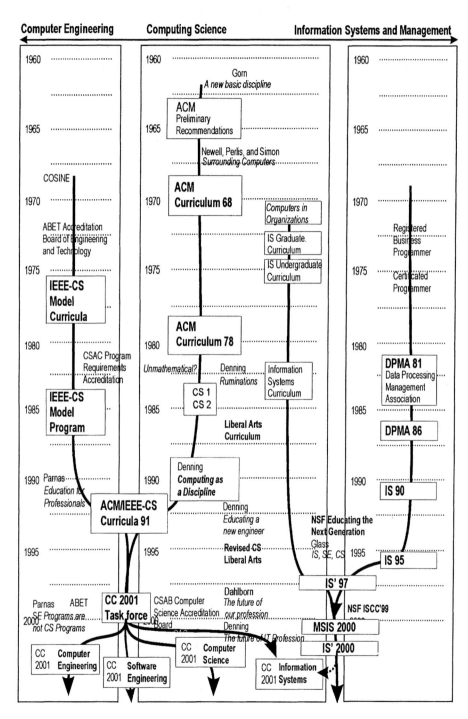

Figure 1. Curricula recommendations in engineering, science, and business

Throughout the consolidation process, most of these fields in Informatics slowly withdrew human and organizational issues from their subject matters, developing perspectives restricted to the artefact, as if it were isolated from its context. In some cases, these issues remained in the domain of particular areas. For example, individuals or groups who were interested in people in Computing Science and in cognition/behavior ended up accommodating their interests in areas such as computer graphics, artificial intelligence, and project management. In Information Systems, the segmentation structured the field into Information Systems and Information Systems Management. Library and Information Science remained outside Informatics as an "application" area, and subdivided into Information Science and Library Science. With time, as the names indicate, each branch negotiated its disciplinary domain and its corresponding organization. Figure 1 does not depict this human dimension, which can be said to be orthogonal to its focus.

Reference to another disciplinary boundary was defended around thirteen years later. In 1967, Newell, Perlis, and Simon wrote a letter to Science, defending the field of Computer Science, explaining its differences, and discussing criticisms. In their definition *"Computer science is the study of the phenomena surrounding computers.* `Computers plus algorithms, `living computers,' or simply computers all come to the same thing - the same phenomena"* [10, 1967, p 1373, added italics]. In terms of disciplinary scope, their definition was narrower than earlier ones. One year later, a more restricted scope can be identified in another definition. In Curriculum 68, a subsequent set of curricula recommendations from the ACM, the committee grouped three major subdivisions that encompassed Computer Science's subject matter [1, pp 154—155]. These three items can be correlated with the later established Computer Engineering, Computing Science, and Information Systems. The ACM committee also chose to label the area Computer Science, instead of information sciences or data management [1 p 153].

The areas mentioned in Curriculum 68 intersected with Mathematics (numerical mathematics and simulation), Engineering (process control), Information Systems (data processing, file management, and information retrieval), and other related areas, such as Philosophy, Linguistics, Industrial Engineering, and Management. The 1968 committee considered them essential to balance Computer Science programs.

The still blurred 1960s computing artefact was clearly subdivided in hardware, software, and systems during the 1970s. This subdivision was accompanied by a disciplinary segmentation chain in which engineers build hardware, computer scientists write software, and information technologists deploy and maintain the resulting systems within organizations. As time passed, educational and professional practices in these fields became increasingly insular. We should stress that the insularity is apparent in terms of disciplinary relations. It worked and it was indeed effective because it has been co-developed with a broader division of labour actualised by other segments. During the 1970s the disciplinary segmentation stabilized. Each specialization became reified across educational institutions and their enacted curricula, across industry and commerce and their organizations, and across governments with policies and resources.

Later on, in Curriculum'78, the committee did not give a definition of Computer Science, but it listed four groups of topics considered fundamental to Computer Science: (a) programming topics, (b) software organization,(c) hardware organization, and, (d) data structures and file processing. In terms of disciplinary relations, this definition enabled (a) a Computer Science focus on programming topics and software organization, (b) an interface with Electrical Engineering through hardware organization, and (c) an interface with Information Systems through data structures and file processing, respectively. We should remark that Curriculum'78 has partially guided the establishment of many Computer Science programs across North America. Curriculum'78 has been criticized for its excessive emphasis on programming. What is usually not mentioned is that, although the core was very narrow and restricted mostly to software, Curriculum'78 had a course on Computers and Society. However, most universities never implemented it.

With the further transformation of Informatics, people started to question the appropriateness of this disciplinary organization. Since the 1980s and 1990s, there have been several attempts to increase, or rescue, some of Informatics' initial breadth and resilience. For example, although Curriculum 68 had several courses in mathematics, Curriculum'78 did not have mathematics in its core set of courses. Its absence was immediately criticized by Ralston and Shaw [12, 13]. As in the Denning report [4, p 16], the excessive emphasis on programming was also criticized in Curricula 91 [2]. The 1991 committee wrote that the emphases given to different topics did not permit a balance between experimental and theoretical computer science [4 , p 9]. A focus on algorithms rather than on programming was an attempt to rescue some of the field's initial orientation. This is clearly stated in Curricula 91.

The 1991 committee also stressed the "basic cultural, social, legal, and ethical issues inherent in the discipline of computing" [2, p 73]. As in Curriculum'78, the 1991 committee did not include such an area in the core courses of computing. The absence of social and ethical issues in Curricula 91 core courses did not pass by without notice. [6] proposed a complementation of Curricula 91, which included social and ethical issues as fundamental, known as the tenth strand. Many other criticisms have been raised throughout the 1990s. Although computer engineers, computing scientists, and information systems technologists shared interests, daily practice had not fostered much interaction among them beyond their established roles and enacted disciplinary interfaces.

It is interesting to note that the emergence of fields such as Software Engineering and Human-Computer Interaction happened during a period in which some specializations in Informatics were acquiring recognition and stability by narrowing their breadth and increasing their depth. Although Software Engineering is often characterized as between Computer Engineering and Computing Science, a close analysis of its proposed body of knowledge unveils a set of topics related to people and organizations such as cognitive science, project management, and management. These topics have been part of Information Systems and Information Systems Management [5, 11].

The emergence of new areas of study, professional occupations, quarrels on established boundaries, inter-disciplinary work, all indicate that Informatics' traditional disciplinary organization is becoming inadequate. There is no recipe to reorganize Informatics, but individuals and committees have already expressed their opinions on how to renew and reorganize the field. In 2000 an IEEE-CS ACM joint task force recognized the "expanding" scope of the profession. Curricula 2001 reflect this concern. The committee has already expressed the view that the sustained narrowing tendencies of prior similar recommendations are currently inadequate. Indeed the task force began its work with a restricted scope of Computing Science and Engineering, as in the Curricula 91.

In Figure 2, disciplinary breadth variations are depicted in relation to the traditional branches of Informatics. The narrowing and expanding tendencies are delimited by two lines. The approximate scopes of several documents have been abstracted to depict the overall dynamics. The ellipses in Figure 2 depict the approximate perspectives adopted by professionals and committees. See Merkle [7] for references. Some professionals, such as David Parnas, tend to reinforce boundaries, others, such as Peter Denning and Wolfgang Coy, tend to blur them. The same can be said about professional associations. The bolder lines depict the approximate Computing Science domain projected on the technical dimension. The lighter lines depict Computer Engineering and Information Systems boundaries. Figure 2 depicts only a small subset of the actual disciplinary diversity present in Informatics. It is limited to three branches and their relations are reduced to a linear scale, which oversimplifies their actual intricate relationships. Other dimensions are required in order to discuss areas such as Human-Computer Interaction and Software Engineering.

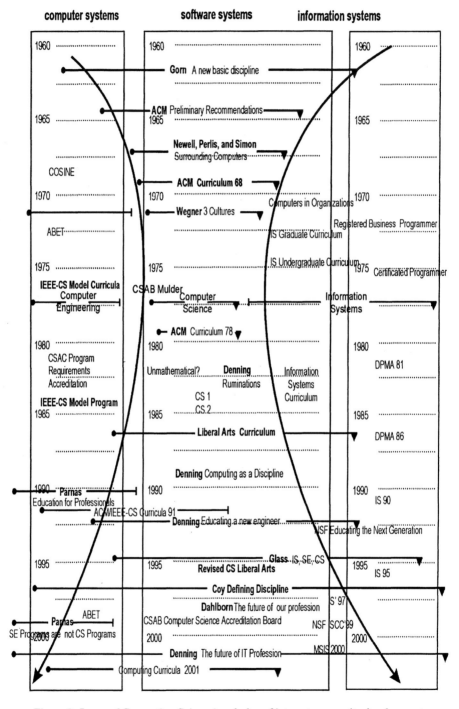

computer systems   **software systems**   **information systems**

Figure 2. Scope of Computing Science's nebulae of interests across its development

3. CONCLUSIONS

The development of a field, a profession, a discipline, a research topic happens not only at its centre or focus, but also on its boundaries and beyond them. However, the successes of Informatics are not enough to justify the over-specialization of its professionals. Current research trends and professional criticisms can be characterized as having or demanding foci that go beyond Informatics' recognized traditional branches. One of the challenges ahead is to overcome the orthodoxy consolidated in professional practices.

The disciplinary diversity found in Informatics' Curricula recommendations suggests that across its initial history several areas and subjects were left out of its concerns. In contrast with the few areas that have been consolidated throughout its development, a myriad of occupations has emerged during the last decade. In 2001, Denning listed thirty-eight areas [3] as part of Information Technology. In this article we have not discussed the reasons behind the inclusion or the exclusion of either the new or the now old.

The future pattern of Informatics' disciplinary development is an open question. The established view would say that it would continue to diversify monotonically, but this is an oversimplification. The short period analysed in this article suggests that the variations may be cyclic. This assumes that only part of the current diversity will develop the required depth that a discipline demands to be consolidated. Areas such as Human-Computer Interaction and Software Engineering give indications that there is cross-pollination with disciplines often housed in the social sciences, such as psychology and management.

Extrapolating the current tendencies, we would speculate that the respective human and process-centred approaches will be consolidated in a next cycle of development, being indeed incorporated into mainstream Informatics. Currently less diffused tendencies are those conjoint with the Arts, and Humanities, such as software design, computer semiotics, and social informatics, among others. It is our opinion that it would be wonderful if the involved communities were able to build bridges between these heterogeneous and usually separate fields. However, taking a conservative but critical stand, we believe that these bridges will demand more than one cycle to be structured and consolidated.

4. ACKNOWLEDGEMENTS

Part of this work was supported by the Brazilian Government through the Conselho Nacional de Pesquisa e Desenvolvimento (CNPq, National Research and Development Council), and by the Canadian Government through the Natural Sciences and Engineering Research Council.

5. REFERENCES

[1] ACM-CCCS. (1968). Curriculum 68: Recommendations for academic programs in Computer Science. *Communications of the ACM*, 11(3):151–197.
[2] ACM/IEEE-CS, J. C. T. F. (1991). Computing Curricula 1991: ACM/IEEE-CS Joint Curriculum Task Force. Technical report, ACM/IEEE.
[3] Denning, P. J. (2001). Who are we? CACM column: IT profession. *Communications of the ACM*, 44(2):11–19.
[4] Denning, P.J., Comer, D.E., Gries, D., Mulder, M.C., Tucker, A., Turner, A.J., and Young, P.R. (1989). Computing as a discipline. *Communications of the ACM*, 32(1):9.
[5] Gorgone, J. T., Gray, P., Feinstein, D. L., Kasper, G. M., Luftaman, J. N., Stohr, E. A., Valacich, J. S., and Wigand, R. T. (1999). MSIS 2000 model curriculum and guidelines for graduate degree programs in Information Systems. Technical report, Association for Computing Machinery (ACM) and Association for Informaiton Systems (AIS).
[6] Martin, C. D., Huff, C., Gotterbarn, D., and Miller, K. (1996). Implementing a tenth strand in the CS curriculum. *Communications of the ACM*, 39(12):75–84.
[7] Merkle, L. E. (2002). *Disciplinary and Semiotic Relations Across Human-Computer Interaction*. Unpublished Ph.D. thesis, The University of Western Ontario - Graduate Program in Computer Science, London, Ontario, Canada.
[8] Mulder, F. and Hacquebard, A. (1998). Specifying and comparing informatics curricula through UCSI. In Mulder, F. and van Weert, T., editors, *Proceedings of IFIP WG3.2 Working Conference on `Informatics' (Computer Science) as a discipline and in other disciplines: what is common?*, London, Chapman & Hall. International Federation for Information Processing.
[9] Mulder, F. and van Weert, T. (2000). IFIP/UNESCO Informatics Curriculum Framework 2000 (ICF 2000). Technical report, International Federation for Information Processing IFIP and UNESCO, Paris.
[10] Newell, A., Perlis, A. J., and Simon, H. A. (1967). Computer Science. *Science* 157(3795):1373–1374.
[11] Nunamaker Jr., J. F., Cougar, J. D., and Davis, G. B. (1982). Information Systems curriculum recommendations for the 80s: Undergraduate and graduate programs - a report on the ACM curriculum committee on Information Systems. *Communications of the ACM*, 25(11):781–805.
[12] Ralston, A. (1984). The first course in Computer Science needs a mathematics corequisite. *Communications of the ACM*, 27(10):1002–1005.
[13] Ralston, A. and Shaw, M. (1980). Curriculum '78 – is Computer Science really that unmathematical? *Communications of the ACM*, 23(2):67–70.
[14] Williams, S. B. (1954). The Association for Computing Machinery *Journal of the Association for Computing Machinery*, 1(1):1–3.

Variety in Views of University Curriculum Schemes for Informatics / Computing / ICT
A comparative assessment of ICF-2000 / CC2001 / Career Space

Fred Mulder, Karel Lemmen, Maarten van Veen
Open University of the Netherlands, Heerlen, The Netherlands, e-mail: fred.mulder@ou.nl,
karel.lemmen@ou.nl, maarten.vanveen@ou.nl

Abstract   Various recognized international professional organizations have recently developed university curricula concepts and models for the broad field which is referred to as computing, informatics or I(C)T (= Information and Communication Technology). The outcomes show a significant diversity, a little maybe because of the difference in terminology but much more so because of a variation in views and approaches. If one expects a strongly grown maturity of the field paralleled by paradigmatic convergence, after so many decades of development, this is a surprising result. In order to gain more insight in this matter this paper presents an assessment exercise for three such curriculum schemes. They are compared on a series of characteristic features as well as judged against a set of general guiding principles. The assessed schemes are ICF-2000 (by IFIP in commission of UNESCO), CC2001 (by ACM and IEEE-CS) and Career Space (by a European consortium of ICT industry in partnership with the European Commission).

Key words: Curriculum models, curriculum guidelines, curriculum assessment, university, higher education, informatics, computing, IT, ICT

1. INTRODUCTION

In 1997 a Working Conference was organized by the Working Group on university education of the International Federation for Information Processing (IFIP). This conference brought together a selected group of experts from all over the world. The conference theme was *"Informatics (computer science) as a discipline and in other disciplines: what is in common?"*. Indeed its focus was on the search for a common vision of the core concepts in education and training in a field that over the past decades has developed, matured, extended, and linked with many other knowledge domains.

This Working Conference was very productive, identified a common core and gave rise to an editorial paper [1]. It summarizes the varying views on the informatics field and comments on the fragmented approach to its teaching. It argues that informatics indeed cannot be forced into a 'monistic' view of normal science such as the 'queen of sciences', physics. Instead, rather than working with more or less isolated paradigms, informatics requires a *'pluralistic' view* in which several paradigms coexist. The editorial paper advocates a more integral, generic and coherent approach, and it presents preliminary notions in a search for a shared identity for the informatics field. It proposes to build and extend on the earlier work of Denning et al. in 1989 [2].

What does this all mean for the university educational arena which meanwhile shows a broad spectrum of informatics studies and educational programmes, varying from generalized to more specialized contents, from theoretical to more applied programmes, and from monodisciplinary to multidisciplinary approaches? Do we observe anything in common, a reasonable level of coherence, and complementary efforts? Is the diversity in focus transparent? These questions are particularly relevant in relation to the recent publication of three major international curriculum efforts:

- *ICF-2000* ('Informatics Curriculum Framework 2000'), for 'informatics' (by IFIP in commission of UNESCO)
- *CC2001* ('Computing Curricula 2001'), for 'computing' (by ACM = Association for Computing Machinery and IEEE-CS = Computer Society of the Institute of Electrical and Electronics Engineers)
- *Career Space* ('Curriculum Development Guidelines / New ICT curricula for the 21st century'), for ICT (by a consortium of eleven major ICT companies within the European Union).
- *Note* that the three terms used are linked to different traditions and communities:
- *'Informatics'* has its roots in academic Europe and is common in IFIP
- *'Computing'* is used in the US to cover 'computer science', 'computer engineering', plus 'information systems' and 'software engineering'
- *ICT* (or just IT in the US) has a more applications oriented connotation and is preferred by industry.

In this paper, they are considered interchangeable umbrella labels.

It is the aim of this paper to *analyse critically* the three curriculum schemes within the context as sketched above of commonality, coherence, complementarity, argued diversity, and transparency. Therefore, we start with a short description of the origins and backgrounds of the three. We then proceed with a first assessment exercise in which we compare the curriculum schemes within a full spectrum of characteristic features, extracted by the authors from the accumulation of the three schemes. A second assessment exercise presents a first-order judgement of the curriculum schemes against a set of eleven principles that guided the CC2001 work. The paper concludes with a discussion on the outcomes and some recommendations.

2. CURRICULUM SCHEMES: ORIGINS AND BACKGROUNDS

In 1998, IFIP was requested by UNESCO to carry out a curriculum project. IFIP's Technical Committee 3 (on Education) adopted the project, which was executed by members of Working Group 3.2 (on Higher Education), complemented with input from other IFIP Technical Committees. The result [3] could be considered a successor of an earlier (1994) IFIP/UNESCO curriculum framework, which however was much narrower in scope (only computer science). *ICF-2000* has its origin in the 1997 IFIP Working Conference mentioned above in that it takes a broad and generic view of the field. It is not a model curriculum but instead offers a *curriculum framework*, designed to cope with the diverse demand for different categories of professionals acting or interacting with informatics. Tailor-made implementations can be constructed from the framework in a straightforward way. An important asset of ICF-2000 is that it contains source links to prominent and current informatics curricula (see also [4]).

The US has a long tradition of developing model curricula for computer science (CS), computer engineering (CE) and information systems (IS). The Curriculum'68 report for CS by ACM was the first in a series. Approximately every decade a new version of the model curriculum has been published: 1968, 1978, 1991, and now the latest report. The 1991 report was a breakthrough, being the result of cooperation between ACM and IEEE-CS elaborating CS and CE, combined in 'computing'. Previously, the two professional societies had followed their own tracks, in which IEEE-CS published a report in 1977 on both CS and CE. The present and forthcoming results under the title *CC2001* represent another *breakthrough* in the ambition to include also IS and SE (software engineering). The first volume (on CS) has been published [5], contains a detailed specification of the curriculum core, and includes rather precise guidelines for variation in curriculum implementation, as well as sample curricula. Other reports (on CE, SE, IS, and an overview document) are scheduled for the future.

Career Space is an initiative, with support of the European Commission, of a consortium of eleven major ICT companies: BT, Cisco Systems, IBM

Europe, Intel, Microsoft Europe, Nokia, Nortel Networks, Philips
Semiconductors, Siemens AG, Telefónica S.A., Thales; furthermore EICTA
(European Information, Communications and Consumer Electronics
Industry Technology Association) is involved. A project was set up to put in
place a clear framework for students, educational institutions and
governments that describes the roles, skills and competencies required by the
ICT industry in Europe. The first step was to develop generic skills profiles
covering the main job areas for which the ICT industry is experiencing skills
shortages [6]. The second step was to develop *new ICT curriculum
guidelines* [7] for which the generic skills profiles are a point of reference. In
the latter project, input came from individual experts from over twenty
European universities and technical institutions. The guidelines are intended
to assist the design of courses to match the skills profiles and needs of
Europe's ICT industry.

3. FIRST ASSESSMENT EXERCISE: COMPARISON OF MAIN CHARACTERISTICS

The *overview* on the following pages compares the three curriculum
schemes along a set of twelve characteristic features. This set has been
inferred by the authors as topical for each of the schemes after a thorough
study of all three. Actually, the overview serves *two functions*:
– it can be read as three parallel stand-alone encyclopedic stories
– it shows the differences and similarities among the curriculum schemes.

*Although we have made a good effort to present a neutral overview, a certain bias
towards ICF-2000 may have slipped in, if only because of the authors'deeper and
first-hand knowledge of ICF-2000. If that happens to be the case, clearly this is not
at all intentional.*

ICF-2000	*CC2001*	*Career Space*
Characteristic feature 1 Umbrella terminology		
Informatics, 'traditionally' referring to a diverse, yet related family of domains: CS = computer science, CE = computer engineering, SE = software engineering, IS = information systems, I(C)T, AI = artificial intelligence, …	*Computing*, originally covering CS and CE, according to Computing Curricula 1991 and [2]. The CC2001 report suggests including also the areas of SE and IS, and maybe others.	*ICT*, Information and Com-munication Technology, which essentially has a very broad connotation. However, by primarily focussing on ICT industry, the scope is less broad.

ICF-2000	*CC2001*	*Career Space*
2 Developing organizations and experts		
The responsible (world) organization is *IFIP*, in particular its Education Technical Committee (TC3). The work was done by a group of IFIP linked experts. The project was commissioned by *UNESCO*, meant to benefit students and institutions in both developed and developing countries.	*ACM* and *IEEE-CS* have produced the 1st volume (CS). The work was done by many experts, with a clear *US base*, though, both in the people and in its context. Additional volumes are to be prepared in consultation with other US based professional societies (SWEEP, AIS, AITP).	A European consortium of *11 ICT companies* (BT, Cisco Systems, IBM Europe, Intel, Microsoft Europe, Nokia, et al) has taken the initiative, in partnership with the *European Commission*. Input was given in a working group by individual experts from over twenty European universities and technical institutions.
3 Status, level of detail and links to other curriculum schemes		
The project was completed in 2000. The comprehensive report offers a rather *global* specification, but includes *links* to various distinguished detailed schemes, such as the CC2001 predecessor (CC1991), IS'97 and ECDL (European Computer Driving Licence).	A 1st volume (on CS) is available since Dec. 2001. Other volumes (on CE, SE, IS, etc.) are foreseen, while an overview document is to complete the series. The CS report is *very detailed* and self contained, not refer-ring to schemes other than its predecessor CC1991.	In 2001 a concise and global report was published. This contains a set of rather *open-ended* recommendations and does not include any reference to other well-known schemes. The report builds, however, on an earlier Career Space report called 'Generic ICT skills profiles' [6].
4 Goal and function		
ICF-2000 offers a *framework* for the *design* of curricula to be implemented in a specific context, given institutional, societal and cultural factors. More specifically, it allows institutions or countries with less developed informatics education to leapfrog to the state-of-the-art.	CC2001 offers a set of *detailed* curriculum *guidelines*, giving a distinct choice from a selected number of model implementations. More specifically, it meets the needs of many US colleges and universities for significant guidance in terms of individual course design.	Career Space offers a set of *global* curriculum development guidelines and *recommendations*, but is not very explicit at implementation. The underlying goal is to narrow the ICT skills gap 'for tomorrow' (and decrease today's shortage) as identified by the ICT industry [6].
5 Paradigmatic view on the field (see also feature 1)		
'Informatics' is viewed broad and generic, basically to be *analysed/decomposed* into domains such as CS, CE, SE, IS, AI, ... This is apparent in its *top-down methodology*: all	*'Computing'* is viewed broad and generic, basically to be *synthesized/composed* from the domains CS and CE (plus - intentionally - SE, IS, ...). This relates to its *bottom-up*	*ICT* is viewed broad and generic, but basically as a *merger* of electrical engineering and informatics, with added business knowledge and behavioural skills. This originates from the

ICF-2000	*CC2001*	*Career Space*
domains are included a priori, advancing coherence and consistency implicitly. This is conditioned by an open and intensive interaction between the scientific communities.	*approach*, yielding separate volumes on the different domains, by the end resulting in a compiled overview document. This requires an explicit mechanism to advance coherence and consistency.	*ICT industry's approach*, trying to solve the ICT skills gap. The report's suggestion that this will also meet the needs of organizations that use ICT intensively does not show.

6 Orientation on demand and supply

ICF-2000 is driven by both *demand* and supply, with a *focus* on the former. It starts from *work force requirements*, identified at a global level. This is done deliberately because of the inevitable difficulty in specifying sustainable precise profiles, also in dialogue with industry.

Eight professionals' categories are distinguished under three main umbrellas:

I(nformatics) users
A1 instrumental
I(nformatics) appliers
B1 conceptual
B2 interfacing
B3 researching
B4 directing
I(nformatics) workers
C1 operational
C2 engineering
C3 researching

To clear this up a little:
- *Instrumental I-users* use I-technology/applications in their work: internet, word processing, graphics, etc.
- *I-appliers* apply I-knowledge/skills in areas different from informatics: a teacher in computer supported education (*conceptual*), a lawyer in software contracts (*interfacing*), a physicist in computational science (*researching*), an information (policy)

CC2001 is primarily driven by *supply*, expressed by *academic requirements*: the identified body of knowledge, undergraduate core material, learning objectives, and detailed course descriptions.

This supply orientation also is apparent in the process that resulted in CC2001/CS. *20 focus groups* supported that process, of which:
- 14 on knowledge areas (typically a supply theme)
- 6 on pedagogical issues across the curriculum:
1 Introductory topics/courses
2 Supporting topics/courses
3 The computing core
4 Professional practices
5 Advanced study and undergraduate research
6 Computing across the curriculum.

Only pedagogy focus group 4 addresses the demand side explicitly. In a chapter dedicated to *professional practice* a few mechanisms are suggested:
- Capstone projects
- Professionalism, ethics, and law courses
- Practicum / internship/ co-op programmes
- Team-based implementation courses.
Elsewhere the report recommends in order to 'complete

Career Space is driven by *demand*, using a set of ICT core generic *skills profiles*, as identified by the ICT industry consortium.

The curriculum report refers to *13 profiles* in the areas [7]:
Telecommunications
1 Radio frequency engineering
2 Digital design
3 Data communications engineering
4 Digital signal processing applications design
5 Communications network design
Software & Services
6 Software & applications development
7 Software architecture and design
8 Multimedia design
9 IT business consultancy
10 Technical support
Products & Systems
11 Product design
12 Integration & test / implementation & test engineering
13 Systems specialist.

In [6] each skills profile is described by a vision / role / lifestyle, as well as by tasks, associated technologies, required skills and career opportunities.

A confrontation with the *supply side* reveals a rather

ICF-2000	CC2001	Career Space
manager (*directing*) - *I-workers* are I-specialists in *operations* (e.g. network operator), systems *design* (e.g. software engineer), or *research* (e.g. postdoc). 　The supply side enters when a best fit to the intended categories of professionals is made through *graduate profiles*, specified in units with targeted competencies and each referring to various curriculum sources.	the curriculum': familiarity with applications, communication skills, working in teams, project courses. 　CC2001 pays measured attention to demand side issues and includes professional practice in its sample curricula. But, the report is also clear on who is to 'rule' the curriculum, namely academic educators.	large mismatch of many running ICT curricula with these profiles. 　*Note* 　Five profiles from [6] have not been included in [7]: ICT marketing management, ICT project management, Research and technology development, ICT management, and ICT sales management. The reason for this is not quite clear.

7 Curriculum core

The curriculum core is taken from [1] and has *12 themes*: 1　Representation of information 2　Formalism in information processing 3　Information modelling 4　Algorithmics 5　System design 6　Software development 7　Potentials and limitations of computing and related technologies 8　Computer systems and architectures 9　Computer-based communication 10　Social and ethical implications 11　Personal and inter-personal skills 12　Broader perspectives and context (including links with other disciplines). 　These twelve core themes constitute each ICF-2000 curriculum. For the eight categories of professionals, however, their relative weight is different (highlighted in so-called theme finger-prints).	The curriculum core is taken from *13* out of 14 *knowledge areas* that span the full CS body of knowledge (no. 14 is Computational science). 　Below we list the core topics, in decreasing order of their % contributions (in brackets) to the curriculum: - Programming fundamentals (19) - Discrete structures (15) - Architecture and organization (13) - Algorithms and complexity (11) - Software engineering (11) - Operating systems (6.5) - Social and professional issues (6) - Net-centric computing (5.5) - Intelligent systems (3.5) - Information management (3.5) - Programming languages (2) - Human-computer interaction (2) - Graphics and visual computing (2). 　The CS report is *strict* on the core: any curriculum	The curriculum core is very *open-ended*. It is considered the university's task to specify those global core components in depth. 　The recommended *4 core components* and their % contributions (in brackets) are: - *Scientific base*, covering the fundamental principles and concepts relevant to ICT industry (30) - *Technology base* with a broad overview of technologies, their functions, advantages and constraints (30) - *Application base and systems thinking* (specialized), giving rise to in-depth knowledge and skills in specialized fields, problem solving skills, and workplace driven application knowledge for particular job profiles (25) - *Personal and business skills*, through team projects, commercial simulations, negotiation, presentation, etc., throughout the curriculum (15). 　The Career Space report indeed is very *liberal* on the

ICF-2000	*CC2001*	*Career Space*
The core themes are manifest in the *curriculum units* by specific patterns. And the units can be leveled at four *competency orientations*: - Awareness (know or use) - Application - Design and modelling - Conceptualization and abstraction.	implementation should contain the *full core* as a minimum. *Note* This is only about the CS core and body of knowledge. Completion with CE, SE and IS is not trivial, at least if a merger with the CS results is intended.	core, guiding to components that are only roughly estimated in student's effort and specified at a high level of abstraction.

8 Curriculum structure and components

The curriculum 'atom' is a *credit point* (cp), standing for about *8 hours of study*. The curriculum is composed of *units* ranging from 2-4 to 9-11 cp. Each unit has a short specification of targeted competencies and references to well-known model curricula. ICF-2000 does *not* combine the units to larger *courses*. The units are clustered in four *'graduate profiles'*: - BIP or *Basic Instrumental* I-Profile (20 cp = 160 hours) - BCP or *Basic Conceptual* I-Profile (40 cp = 320 hours) - MIP or *MInor* I-Profile (80 cp = 640 hours) - MAP or *MAjor* I-Profile (160 cp = 1280 hours). Each profile is 80% generic, 20% specific. These profiles build one upon the other and meet the needs of the eight professionals' categories A1-C3 (feature 6): - BIP is meant for *all students*, a 3% part in a 3-year bachelor programme (A1) - BCP + BIP, a 10% bachelor part, offers a flexible fit for a large volume of *students in*	The curriculum 'atom' is the conventional *lecture hour* (lh) which should be interpreted as *4 hours of study* in order to include out-of-class study. The curriculum is composed of *units* ranging from 1 to 14 lh. These units are contained in *courses* that in the report are assumed to have a typical size of: 40 lh = 160 hours. Courses are *clustered* in different arrangements, each specifying - by a particular implementation strategy - a full component of a model undergraduate *(bachelor)* CS programme. Three *course levels* are distinguished: introductory, intermediate and advanced. The advanced courses go well beyond the core, but within the 14 knowledge areas. CC2001/CS contains a considerable set of detailed CS *course descriptions*. The report recommends to *complete* the undergraduate CS curricula with *non-core requirements* in: - Mathematical rigor - Scientific method	Career Space does *not* define a *metris* to measure curriculum components in terms of curriculum 'atoms' or other units. Nor does it specify course contents. Career Space applauds the European *'Bologna' approach*. It adopts the higher education structure of a 1st cycle programme of 3-4 years *(bachelor* degree) and a 2nd cycle programme of 1-2 years *(master* degree). The report suggests a *hierarchical* generic structure for 1st cycle ICT curricula, embracing the full core: - Year 1: *general core* modules - Year 2: *area-specific* core and *elective* modules - Year 3-4: *specialization* and *advanced* topics, plus about 15% of the curriculum for *practical work* experience (industry placement of 3 months) and *bachelor project* thesis work (3 months). The 2nd *cycle* should contain *advanced* topics in the same *four core areas* as for the 1st cycle. And again an industry placement, plus a master thesis (in total up to

ICF-2000	CC2001	Career Space

non-informatics studies (B1)
- MIP + BCP + BIP is for students in a *non-informatics bachelor* who want to incorporate informatics in their study (up to almost a quarter) with a certain degree of *specialization* (B2-B4)
- MAP + MIP + BCP + BIP, adding up to 2400 hours, about half a *bachelor* programme in *informatics*, including a 20% specialization, 10% electives and 12.5% required projects (C1-C3).
	- Applications familiarity
	- Communication skills
	- Team working (projects)
	- Employment empowering.
	   The *sample curricula* show room for elective courses (around 10%) and a capstone project (also around 10%).
	   The size of the core is 280 lh = 1120 hours.
	For the other components mentioned the size depends on the implemented model.
		40% of the curriculum).
		   The report observes a need to *cluster* the 13 skills profiles (feature 6) into, for example, *three separate curricula*:
		- Information Technology (skills profiles 1, 2, 4 and 10)
		- Computer Science (profiles 6, 7 and 9)
		- Integrated curriculum (other skills profiles).

9 Transfer of subjects and concepts from other disciplines

In each graduate profile, *20%* has been reserved for units that are *discipline specific*. These are meant to be inter-disciplinary in approach.
   ICF-2000 also refers to a wide variety of *non-informatics subjects* that may be relevant for a specific curriculum implementation. This, however, has not been further detailed.
   The ICF-2000 body of knowledge is restricted to informatics; no other disciplines elements are included.
	CC2001 recommends to *include* in the CS curriculum:
	- Discrete mathematics
	- Selected additional maths. subjects (calculus, etc.)
	- Science/scientific method
	- An application domain.
	   The CS body of knowledge *includes* two strictly spoken *non-computing* areas: discrete structures and computational science. It is not clear what this 'inclusive' approach implies when the CS body of knowledge will be completed with CE, SE and IS, for which other non-computing areas are relevant.
		Career Space draws heavily on *non-ICT* areas, supposing a *strong link* and cohesion with the ICT domain itself. This holds for the following components:
		- Scientific base
		- Application base
		- Personal and business skills.
		   The report does not present any further detail as to what content is to be incorporated and how the integration with the ICT domain can be achieved.

10 Transfer to other disciplines' curricula

Inherent to its design of four graduate profiles, ICF-2000 addresses the issue of *'Informatics for all'* explicitly.
   Implementation is possible at *three levels*:
- for virtually all students BIP should be compulsory
- in many bachelor programmes BCP should be required
- on top of that MIP prefer-
	CC2001 contains a chapter on *'Computing across the curriculum'*, which refers to a key NRC report [8]. This report identifies computer-specific *skills*, fundamental and enduring computing *concepts*, and general *intellectual capabilities*, that all should be included in general undergraduate education.
	   CC2001 recommends *three*
		Career Space does *not* address the issue of *'ICT in any other study'*.

ICF-2000	*CC2001*	*Career Space*
ably would be chosen as an option by many students.	*course models*: general fluency, multi-disciplinary, single discipline specializing.	

11 Variety in implementation

Implementation variety with a broad scope is an essential quality of ICF-2000. This is effected by the *framework's degrees of freedom*, such as the:
- diversity in the links with the professionals' categories
- graduate profile options
- discipline context
- competency orientations
- built-in spread in individual unit sizes
- curriculum sources.
  The report contains a separate chapter on *implementation factors* (institutional, societal, cultural, available resources, etc.) and suggested *strategies*.
	Implementation variety is considered necessary, shaped primarily by the suggested *strategies*:
	- at *introductory* level: impe-rative-, objects-, functional-, breadth-, algorithms-, and hardware-first
	- at *intermediate* level: topic-based, compressed, systems-based, and web-based.
	  CC2001 suggests *three sample CS curricula*, i.e. for research-oriented universities (in the US), single discipline focused universities (e.g. in Europe), and liberal arts colleges with a small CS department (in the US).
	  The report concludes with a chapter on relevant *institu-tional factors*.
		Implementation variety is very large because of the *global* level of specification and the *liberal* approach to curriculum design.
		  With an explicit focus on the ICT industry's needs, Career Space advocates a close *collaboration* between *stake-holders* inside and outside the university. They should all be involved in design, control and operation of the university education process, in four steps:
		- set up entry requirements
		- define outcomes (graduate qualifications)
		- define the education and assessment process
		- implement curriculum quality control.

12 Updating mechanism

Ongoing updating is con-sidered essential. ICF-2000 has been designed in such a way that this is *relatively simple*. New versions of model curricula can replace earlier ones by just updating references in ICF-2000. Also new curricula may be added to the framework with relatively little effort.
  An updating mechanism is proposed, however not effect-ive, since there is no active core group of committed IFIP or other experts working on the project any more.
	Ongoing updating is advo-cated rather than what hap-pened before, once a decade.
	  It is *not clear* from the report how this will be *established*.
	Also, it is unknown how the *future* curriculum develop-ment for CE, SE and IS, and the overview document, will *influence* the current CS outcomes. Presupposing better overall coherence and consistency as a final result, it is hard to imagine that there would be no impact on the CS body of knowledge, its core and curriculum content.
		Career Space does *not* address the *necessity* of updating explicitly, maybe because the dominant current interest is implementation anyway.
		  But of course regular feed-back and updating is a must. It is not clear from the report whether Career Space will organize such a follow-up.

4. SECOND ASSESSMENT EXERCISE: SCORES ON GUIDING PRINCIPLES

The *overview* below judges the three curriculum schemes against a set of eleven principles that guided the CC2001 work. We have chosen this set because it reflects a *state-of-mind* that in our view is more or less generic. It seemed appropriate to conform to this set, at least in a first attempt. However, to facilitate a really generic approach to all three schemes we had to make two *'editorial' changes* in the CC2001 guiding principles:
- the term 'computer science' has been replaced by the more generic term 'computing' (in this paper synonymous to 'informatics' and to ICT)
- all specific references to CC2001 have been substituted by a generic reference to 'curriculum scheme'.

The overview shows a set of scores for each of the curriculum schemes on a scale varying from + + to − −. The scores indicate the extent to which the *principles apply* to the scheme and are assigned by the authors. The motivation for the scoring is attached to each principle and is rooted in the descriptions of the characteristic features in the previous section.

Notes
- Like in the previous section, we note that there may - unintentionally - be bias (or misinterpretation) in the results, since our judgement has not been validated with the developers of CC2001 and Career Space. Hence, what we see here should be considered as provisional, first-order.
- For CC2001 the score sometimes is split into an actual one (referring to the CS report published so far) and - in brackets - a future perspective one (assuming all anticipated reports being available).

Guiding principle	ICF-2000	CC2001	Career Space
1/ *Computing is a broad field that extends well beyond the boundaries of computer science.*	+ +	− [+ +]	0

Motivation   [refer to characteristic features 1, 3, 5]
This becomes manifest definitely in ICF-2000. CC2001 in its present version is restricted to CS, so naturally does not go beyond CS (scoring a −), but when the additional volumes appear CC2001's score perspective is + +. The Career Space report so far shows a limited scope on ICT, but certainly broader than CS.

2/ *Computing draws its foundations from a wide variety of disciplines.*	+ / −	+ / −	+ / −

Motivation   [refer to characteristic features 7, 9]
All three schemes conform to this principle with compulsory curriculum components that treat relevant issues from other disciplines, either themselves or integrated with areas of the computing discipline. Hence, the principle is visible (score +), but in none of the schemes this has led to a level of elaboration that could yield a clear-cut implementation (score −).

Guiding principle	*ICF-2000*	*CC2001*	*Career Space*
3/ The rapid evolution of computing requires an ongoing review of the corresponding curriculum.	+ + / 0	+ + / –	0

Motivation   *[refer to characteristic feature 12]*
ICF-2000 and CC2001 both are outspoken on this principle (score + +), but the score is reduced by the lack of an operational guarantee. For ICF-2000 which by its design actually offers simplicity for updating, the score is lowered to 0. For CC2001 where updating is complicated by the expected interference with the forthcoming curriculum developments for CE, SE and IS, the score is lowered to –. Career Space is not explicit on this principle.

4/ Development of a computing curriculum must be sensitive to:			
- changes in technology	+	+	+
- new developments in pedagogy	–	–	– –
- the importance of lifelong learning.	–	–	–

Motivation   *[refer to characteristic features 6, 11, 12]*
All schemes account for adaptation to changes in technology, partly by allowing flexibility in the exploitation of the curriculum, partly by an ongoing updating mechanism.
Pedagogical issues are addressed in ICF-2000 and CC2001, however in a rather conventional context: nothing 'to the point' about competency-based, problem-based, project-based learning, and nothing about e-learning, portfolio learning and learning communities. Career Space is poor in this respect, paying almost no attention to pedagogical issues (score – –). None of the schemes incorporates operational mechanisms in view of (the preparation for) lifelong learning; indeed they all concentrate on the traditional undergraduate track.

5/ The curriculum scheme must go beyond knowledge units to offer significant guidance in terms of individual course design.	–	+ +	– –

Motivation   *[refer to characteristic features 3, 4, 8, 11]*
CC2001 excels on this principle. ICF-2000 does not score well, but indeed, it does not aim to offer such detail. It deliberately leaves such an elaboration to those who implement, at the same time choosing for institutional flexibility and appropriateness for some dynamic change. Career Space is even 'worse' and clearly does not comply with this principle at all.
Note that if one would invert principle 5 (as ICF-2000 and Career Space seem to do), all scores should be negated (– becomes + and vice versa), turning round the overall picture.

6/ The curriculum scheme should seek to identify the fundamental skills and knowledge that all computing students must possess.	+	– [+]	–

Motivation   *[refer to characteristic features 5, 6, 7]*
CC2001 in its present version is only about CS, which implies a limited view on the fundamental skills and knowledge (scoring a –). The CC2001 approach as such, however, arouses expectations of a more inclusive picture when the other volumes are available, hence a + in perspective. For ICF-2000 principle 6 is a major driver (scoring a +). Career Space scores a –, because it also has to grow towards more inclusiveness and does not offer much guidance.

Guiding principle	ICF-2000	CC2001	Career Space
7/ The required body of knowledge must be made as small as possible.	+	+ [–]	0

<u>Motivation</u>   *[refer to characteristic features 7, 9]*
ICF-2000 uses a restricted set of 12 core themes for the broad field 'informatics', containing no elements from other disciplines. CC2001/CS also uses a limited body of 14 CS knowledge areas (of which 2 would be more appropriate within mathematics). Future completion with CE, SE and IS undoubtedly will lead to a substantial enlargement into a broadly covering body of knowledge. Therefore the score (a + for CS), will probably go down in perspective (set to a –). Career Space is open-ended and refers to a really small number of core components, of very global quality however; it does not incorporate any structure that could be considered a body of knowledge.

| *8/ The curriculum scheme must strive to be international in scope.* | + | 0 | 0 |

<u>Motivation</u>   *[refer to characteristic features 2, 3, 4, 11]*
Career Space has a European base, although all ICT companies involved are also present outside Europe. CC2001 is predominantly US-based, but incidentally makes an excursion outside North America. ICF-2000 probably is principally most global in scope, facilitated by its linking to distinguished curriculum schemes from whatever continent or country.

| *9/ The development of the curriculum scheme must be broadly based.* | 0 | 0 | + |

<u>Motivation</u>   *[refer to characteristic features 2, 6]*
This principle implies participation by various constituencies from higher education as well as industry and government. Career Space satisfies this approach best: its origin is in industry, a number of universities supplied input, and the European Commission is involved. CC2001 and ICF-2000 both have a broad basis, but only in academia.

| *10/ The curriculum scheme must include professional practice as an integral component of the undergraduate curriculum.* | + | 0 | + + / 0 |

<u>Motivation</u>   *[refer to characteristic features 6, 8]*
All three schemes appear to have applied this principle seriously. The strongest advocate is Career Space which actually considers professional practice as the main driver for arranging the curriculum (score + +). However, the report does not offer much guidance for its implementation (score lowered to 0). The different scores for ICF-2000 and CC2001 stem from the difference in orientation: demand (professionals) versus supply (academia) driven.

| *11/ The curriculum scheme must include discussions of strategies and tactics for implementation along with high-level recommendations.* | + | + | + |

<u>Motivation</u>   *[refer to characteristic features 8, 11]*
All three reports contain a separate chapter in line with this principle and give guidance with recommendations. The implementation space as such, however, differs among the three curriculum schemes from micro- to macro-level variety.

5. DISCUSSION

We may *conclude* as follows.
- ICF-2000, CC2001 and Career Space are all substantial curriculum efforts of recognized organizations and committed experts, aiming at impact in an international context.
- These curriculum schemes show similarities, but also distinct differences.
- Strong points of one scheme could set aside weak points of another scheme. For example, the focus on the demand side in Career Space could compensate the missing attention for demand aspects in CC2001; or the deep level of elaboration of CC2001 could support ICF-2000 and Career Space in which this is lacking; or the broad top-down view on the field of ICF-2000 could contribute to CC2001 and Career Space.
- The schemes share a long term ambition, namely a coherent educational programming with diversity in a matured and broad field of informatics/computing/ICT, linked to a wide variety of other disciplines.
- A separate track approach has been dominant so far, but international interaction around the three schemes could - in the long run - create a mutually beneficial way of working, a quality impetus and increased international transparency for both students and employers.
- The two assessments offer useful first-order instruments for bringing the process further of increasing transparency, maturity and quality of higher education in informatics/computing/ICT, building on a variety of views, perspectives, interests and needs.

Two earlier conferences offered a good opportunity to share visions on university informatics/computing curricula from the ACM/IEEE-CS and IFIP perspectives: the 1997 IFIP/WG3.2 Working Conference referred to in the introduction [1] and the 7th IFIP World Conference on Computers in Education WCCE2001 in Denmark. At this conference, both CC2001 and ICF-2000 were presented and discussed. A try-out comparative analysis of the two (see [4]) gave rise to a lively debate and a better understanding of qualities and complementarity of the various activities.

In that context we end this paper with the following *recommendations*.
- The two curriculum assessments introduced in this paper should be upgraded from exercise level to acknowledged quality. First, this concerns the assessment items themselves for which input from CC2001 and Career Space could lead to a broadly based agreement on the instruments. Second, the results should be validated by CC2001 and Career Space on both the characteristic features and the guiding principles scores.
- It would be an interesting discovery tour with probably a large added value to join forces in common projects at themes that definitely need

further development and implementation in all initiatives. One could think of 'informatics for all/computing across the curriculum', search for a shared identity of the field (merger of paradigms, common core), shift from knowledge-oriented towards competency-based learning, etc.

– In two other areas collaborative efforts seem to be relevant. The first one is on curriculum updating and innovation, which is required in all initiatives but - as it seems - not yet effectively incorporated. The second one is on curriculum implementation in institutions or countries with a less developed higher education programming on informatics/ computing/ICT, for example in developing countries.

6. REFERENCES

[1] Mulder, F., van Weert, T.J. [eds] (1998) *Informatics in higher education: Views on informatics and non-informatics curricula*, Proceedings IFIP/WG3.2 Working Conference. London, Chapman & Hall. (The editorial paper is entitled 'Towards informatics as a discipline: search for identity', pages 3-10.)

[2] Denning, P.J., Comer, D.E., Gries, D., Mulder, M.C., Tucker, A.B., Turner, A.J., Young, P.R. (1989) Computing as a discipline. *Communications of the ACM*, **32** (1), 9-23.

[3] Mulder, F., van Weert, T.J. [eds] (2000*) ICF-2000: Informatics Curriculum Framework 2000 for higher education.* Paris, UNESCO / IFIP. URL:http://www.ifip.or.at/pdf/ICF2001.pdf.

[4] Mulder, F., van Weert, T.J. (2001) IFIP/UNESCO's Informatics Curriculum Framework 2000 for higher education. *SIGCSE Bulletin - inroads*, **33** (4), 75-83.

[5] Cross II, J.H., Engel, G., Roberts, E., Shackelford, R. [co-chairs Joint IEEE-CS & ACM Task Force on Computing Curricula] (2001) *Computing Curricula 2001: Computer Science*. Los Angeles / New York, IEEE Computer Society / Association for Computing Machinery. URL: http://www.acm.org/sigcse/cc2001/cc2001.pdf.

[6] Career Space (2001) *Generic ICT skills profiles: future skills for tomorrow's world.* Luxembourg (Office for Official Publications of the European Communities), CEDEFOP (European Centre for the Development of Vocational Training) / Career Space. URLs: http://www.career-space.com and http://www.cedefop.gr.

[7] Career Space (2001) *Curriculum development guidelines / New ICT curricula for the 21st century: designing tomorrow's education.* Luxembourg (Office for Official Publications of the European Communities), CEDEFOP (European Centre for the Development of Vocational Training) / Career Space. URLs: http://www.career-space.com and http://www.cedefop.gr.

[8] National Research Council / Committee on IT Literacy (1999) *Being fluent with Information Technology.* Washington DC, National Academy Press. URL: http://www. nap.edu/catalog/6482.html.

REPORTS OF THE WORKING GROUPS

Directions and Challenges in Informatics Education

John Hughes (Chairperson)[AUS] Andrew McGettrick (Rapporteur)[UK]
Participants:

Ellen Francine Barbosa[BR], Jens Kaasboll[NO], Vinicius Medina Kern[BR], Ana Paula Ludtke Ferreira[BR], Esselina Macome[MZ], Joberto Martins[BR], Clara Amelia de Oliveira[BR], Alfonso Ignacio Orth[BR], R. Sadananda[TH], Elaine da Silva[BR], Romero Tori[BR]

Abstract: The role of this working group is to focus on examples of recent efforts to address current challenges in teaching informatics, and also to identify future challenges in informatics education. (The term 'informatics' is seen here to be broad and inclusive.

1. DISCUSSION SUMMARY

1.1 The Current State of Informatics Education

1.1.1 Curricular Developments

There have been a number of recent notable curricular developments in informatics. These include
- Curriculum 2001 and in particular the Computer Science volume; there is a related volume for two-year colleges in the US but also the promise of complementary volumes on Software Engineering, Computer Engineering, and Information Systems.

- The IFIP / UNESCO curriculum ICF-2000; This is not a model curriculum, but a curriculum framework that contains links to other prominent and current informatics curricula

An important facet of these initiatives is that they have sought (with varying degrees of success) to be international in nature; this is to be interpreted to mean that they offer curricular advice of relevance to many countries.

Other developments of a national nature are also occurring. In Brazil, for example, the Ministry of Education has provided a framework in the form of curricular directives – essentially guidelines – for certain kinds of programs. These include computer science, computer engineering, information systems and a further pedagogical strand. Within these strands, there are certain required topics but there is scope for local variation and specialisation. Further input to curricular details is provided from the Brazilian Computer Society. As in Australia, the advice here takes the form of accreditation guidance, which mandates a clear set of objectives, a certain breadth as well as a portion (e.g. one third) of the material at an advanced level and all this within a properly resourced environment. There is a body of knowledge and certain basic requirements of all programs: transferable skills, professional issues, societal impact, quality concerns, and project management.

1.1.2 Quality Issues

These curricular developments can be seen as one approach, a constructive approach, to quality. By defining advice and guidance on curricular matters, appropriate support is provided for curricular developers; this has the effect of setting expectations and providing points of reference.

Related to, but distinct from the above, are developments related to the quality of programs. These include benchmarking standards for Computing in the UK. Certain countries (for example, Australia and the UK) have the concept of a qualifications framework which captures a range of qualifications and, in support of life long learning, this provides encouragement for individuals to acquire ever higher qualifications.

A third approach to quality is about to be used in informatics in Brazil. A national examination for graduates of informatics programs is to be implemented. This already exists in the more popular disciplines, e.g. engineering, administration, the law. The examination is mandatory for all students and there is pressure from institutions for students to perform well since success is seen as a hallmark of the best institutions. Indeed the results of such examinations are used to rank institutions. In the Brazilian context it is currently unclear whether there will one examination for the whole field of informatics or one examination per strand; in either case there are concerns in Brazil about the possibility of stifling diversity. However, at higher levels, this entire process is seen as encouraging quality.

Additional approaches to quality include accreditation activities by professional bodies and government boards, and customs such as the external examiner system in the UK and Norway; recently there have been signs of this role being further enhanced in the UK. In some parts of the world, licensing and certification are also important quality indicators.

1.1.3 Use of Curricular Developments

The manner in which published curricula such as CC2001 are used outside of the United States varies. Many institutions tend to see such documents as points of reference. Thus, they tend to adopt good features but do not accept the recommendations blindly. An important aspect here is the recognition that, for instance, the needs of the United States and the needs of countries such as Brazil are different; accordingly. the university curricula ought to reflect this.

2. TRENDS IN INFORMATICS EDUCATION

2.1 Growth Issues

The number of programs has increased in all countries. In some countries the number of degree titles is controlled by government edict, but in others – such as the UK and Australia where market forces operate – the diversity of course provision has also increased dramatically.

There has been an expansion in the number of institutions and organisations offering courses and qualifications. In part, this has been a response to the need for certain skills to be acquired in a short time. Traditional universities have had to address foundational issues and this has frequently prevented rapid response to market demands. Organisations, including major hardware and software providers, have therefore moved to fill the gaps (niche markets). These organisations are, by their very nature, transantional and provide qualifications that are a form of international currency. In other places existing organisations have introduced new 'fast track" programs often with support from government. In Brazil, for instance, the concept of the 'sequential program' (sequential) is one such development in universities that already offer full degree programs.

3. CHANGES OF EMPHASIS TOWARDS LEARNING

There has been a shift in emphasis towards learning and away from teaching. Thus the role of the teacher changes to "the guide on the side" and no longer "the sage on the stage". This is manifest in an emphasis on learning outcomes and competency. Students are now more aware of these issues and, ideally of what is expected of them. Activities such as problem solving foster a focus on active learning. The teacher needs to pay greater attention to setting goals to extend the horizons of students and to set expectations. The concept of such induction is of growing importance. Educational techniques such as peer review might be used to stimulate students to assume responsibility for their learning.

These developments can be seen as important support for life long learning. They are not the only pre-requisites since fundamentally life long learning can be interpreted as stemming from an attitude of mind. This needs to be fostered by approaches to learning and teaching that continually challenge the student around the forefronts of knowledge and development.

The rate of change in the discipline is such that, for the foreseeable future, there will be need for professionals to continuously keep up-to-date. Once in employment, learning often needs to occur over a short time frame. There are apparent contradictions here – life long learning, short term needs and requirements.

4. CHANGES IN THE DISCIPLINE

There has been no decrease in the rate of change within the discipline. However, with the many new developments it is important to identify changes that appear to be occurring within the discipline of informatics. In some courses, there does appear to be a de-emphasis in the importance of programming; in such courses there tends to be an emphasis on the use of packages and of tools.

Although change continues to take place, there is an increasing consensus on the nature of the core of certain parts of the curriculum, e.g. computer science.

Another important trend is towards greater emphasis on curricula that integrate informatics with other disciplines (interdisciplinarity or multi-disciplinarity).

5. TRANSFERABLE SKILLS

Basically, the era of the asocial programmer has come to an end. Thus there is greater need in all programs for interpersonal skills. In the context of informatics these are particularly important to extract requirements, to learn from others, to teach and explain to others, to form part of a group or a team, and so on. The development of additional skills including critiquing and negotiation needs to be addressed.

It is no longer adequate for graduates in informatics to possess only technical skills. They also need to possess skills that recognise the social, legal, ethical and professional context in which they work, and they need to be aware of their responsibilities.

6. FACULTY PERSPECTIVES

The increased attention on quality concerns and the changing emphasis on learning has created faculty who are now more concerned with learning and teaching. Thus, awards and rewards for quality have had a beneficial effect.

There remain considerable problems in attracting well qualified staff into informatics, and in particular into such areas as information systems and communications.

7. STUDENT INTEREST

Retention rates within informatics seem to be a problem in all countries, with some situations being more acute than others.

8. CHALLENGES IN INFORMATICS EDUCATION

8.1 Internationalisation

The discussion on internationalisation of curricula is important. However, this needs to address directly the following question: from a curricular perspective, a key aim for many countries is to produce graduates who are internationally competitive. The reasons for this relate to the global economy, to open markets, to multinational companies, to trends such as the outsourcing of software, to the nature of the software and computing industries, to employment. and fundamentally to the confidence of new graduates. Without this, any country runs the risk of jobs being taken up by graduates from abroad, of losing industry to other countries and so on.

What does internationalisation mean in practice? Clearly, advances such as CC2001 and the ICF 2000 curriculum are crucial in this regard but some additional insights are needed. To reiterate, the blind adoption of these published curricula is often not an entirely sensible approach. These have been successful to a large degree in their attempts to eliminate cultural bias but this is only one step on the pathway to the internationalisation of the curriculum.

An aspect of internationalisation relates to the use of the English language, the lingua franca of the informatics field. Textbooks and other important materials are commonly in English. It is important to recognise that, for difficult topics, the use of English presents an additional hurdle to learning at all levels. Currently in many countries, postgraduate courses are often delivered in English.

A modest but important contribution would be a standardisation of terms such as 'course', 'class', 'program', 'credit systems', etc.

This internationalisation matter merits considerable further thought and attention.

9. CURRICULAR DEVELOPMENTS

The nature of the CC2001 effort is such that, wisely, the CC2001 steering committee did not unduly constrain the teams involved in developing software engineering, computer engineering, etc. With the publication of the final volumes there will be a challenge to evaluate the resulting documents with a view to determining best practice in terms of curricular design. From this there should emerge guidance on matters such as how best to provide a body of knowledge. Part of the considerations here will include the logistics associated with the difficult task of keeping published curricula up-to-date. Of course, there is a related issue of approaches to curricular design that facilitate keeping an individual institution's offerings up-to-date.

It would be a mistake to assume that the curricula emerging here will meet all of the community's needs. Undoubtedly further developments will be required; for instance in Australia there are courses on multimedia and e-commerce that do not sit well with these developments. However, there just has to be some economy of effort. It must be possible to build on these foundational efforts without the investment of many person-years of effort.

Therein lies another challenge.

10. INDUSTRIAL CONCERNS

With recent changes in the computing and informatics industries, one of the challenges now facing educators is having to produce graduates for a dynamic, volatile and uncertain industry sector.

11. DELIVERY OF THE CURRICULUM

In terms of the delivery of the curriculum, (and perhaps even access to it) those involved in informatics teaching often do not use technology itself to increase the efficiency and effectiveness of their efforts. In this regard, developments in e-learning are relevant.

In this context Seymour Papert's comment that 'any teacher who can be replaced by a computer should be' is highly relevant. Greater attention to learning strategies must be beneficial.

Success in the development of teaching materials is most common when an individual uses material for their own class; when material is used by another the success rate tends to fall off dramatically; a further stage is reached with publication and then the success rate is even smaller. Part of the problem here is the effort and commitment (time, effort and resources) needed to produce material that is sufficiently flexible yet useful and reliable.

In 1997, at the IFIP WG3.2 Working Conference held at the University of Twenty, the key issues around the (then) current state of informatics education were identified as:-
- an ongoing identity crisis for informatics
- a danger of isolation, with informatics being internally focused, to the exclusion of the needs of its domains of application
- changing roles for informatics graduates as software technologies develop
- changing learning environments (to more flexible student-centred approaches)
- an increasingly global information infrastructure.

Recent curriculum initiatives have gone a long way towards resolving the identity crisis. The demand to avoid isolation has grown, with increasing trends towards interdisciplinery curricula in areas such as bioinformatics and enviro(nmental infor)matics. The other issues are as relevant today (and possibly no closer to resolution) as they were in 1997.

12. FUTURE DIRECTIONS

It has to be important to encourage experimentation with new approaches to curricular design and to new ways of teaching informatics. The current problems of retention are testimony to the fact that many people wish to become skilled in informatics, but are being turned off. Generally, the economies of many countries require people with these important skills. Developments such as

– experimenting with the use of games for learning and teaching
– the development of interpersonal skills early in the curriculum

are to be encouraged but it is important that, for example, negative gender issues do not appear. Basically new and more effective approaches to learning are needed.

In this context, one future direction may be to teach informatics to students who do not possess the normally expected mathematical skills. Some would argue that mathematical requirements are often grossly overstated, and a more limited mathematical agenda can be taught in the context of informatics. Is it the mathematics that is needed, or is it the formal and logical reasoning that underpins both informatics and mathematics that is important? There is also merit in seeing a distinction between mathematics and logical reasoning; many aspects of the latter can be conveniently - and more meaningfully, from an informatics perspective - taught in the context of programming. There is a challenge in devising curricula that reflect the abilities of students rather than impose impediments to study.

Although many would claim a decrease in mathematical ability of students, this is often accompanied by an increase in language ability; this appears to be the case in Norway.

To support many of these challenges and initiatives it will be important to have appropriate quality measures in the background to guard against ill-conceived developments. A judgement has to be made here as to whether the current and evolving quality standards are indeed appropriate; they must not be excessively bureaucratic and they must not stifle development.

At the end of the day, those involved with these matters must think deeply and sympathetically about future generations of young aspiring informatics students.

13. REFERENCES

[1] Mulder, F. and van Weert, T.J. (editors) *IFIP / Unesco's Informatics Curriculum Framework for Higher Education*, SIGCSE Bulletin – inroads, 33 (4), 75-83.

[2] Roberts, E. and Engels, G. (editors) *Computing Curriculum 2001 – the Computer Science, Final Report*, published by ACM and IEEE, December, 2001.

[3] Comissao de Especialistas de Ensino de Computacao e Informatica – *CEEInf, Diretrizes Curriculares de Cursos da Area de Computacao e Informatica*, 1999.

[4] Sociedade Brasiliera de Computacao (1999) *Curriculo de referencia da SBC para Cursos de Graduacao em Computacao*, versao 1999. Available online at www.sbc.org.br/educacao)

[5] Australian Computer Society, *Core Body of Knowledge*, (available at www.acs.org.au)

Teaching Programming and Problem Solving: The Current State

Elliot Koffmann (US, chair), Torsten Brinda (GER, Rapporteur)

Participants

Juan Alvarez (CL), Amruth Kumar (US), Maria Lucia Blanck Lisboa (BR), Juris Reinfelds (US), Peter Van Roy (BE), Raul Sidney Wazlawick (BR).

1. PARADIGMS AND LANGUAGES

Several approaches are currently used for introductory courses in Informatics. For example the ACM 2001 Curriculum report presents a choice of paradigms for the introductory programming courses: imperative first, objects early, objects first, functional first. These courses are taught in a variety of programming languages, most notably Java, C, C++ and in the recent past Pascal. Normally one language is used in the programming courses. The Advanced Placement Examination in the US and Informatics departments in many countries are transitioning to Java due to its practical relevance and support of object-oriented programming. In some institutions, the introductory programming sequence is expanding from a two-course to a three-course sequence, e.g. programming basics, object-oriented programming (OOP), data structures and algorithms (DS+AL) or OOP1, OOP2, DS+AL.

2. PROBLEMS

Diversity of student background

In the introductory courses, the teachers have to cope with very different pre-knowledge of their students. Some students start with an excellent secondary education in Informatics, others have acquired a lot of knowledge in their spare time or in jobs on the side, others come with hardly any pre-knowledge. Some students who have experience will need to unlearn bad habits. Moreover, many students start their Informatics studies with insufficient mathematical and logical thinking capabilities and they have difficulty with the abstractions needed for success in Informatics. A lot of them also have incorrect expectations about Informatics study.

Students without prior experience

Some students without any prior computing experience will outperform those who have prior experience. We need to make sure that students without experience are not discouraged from taking introductory programming courses. We also need to keep in mind that learning programming in college is a new experience for these students. For example, they have all taken History and Mathematics courses, but many of them have no experience in learning how to solve problems or in algorithmic thinking.

Faculty resource and training

The dropout rate in the introductory courses is high. However, this is not just because of problems on the side of the students. Faculty shortages are a big problem that often leads to non Computer-Science-trained faculty, or faculty without an object-oriented background, teaching introductory courses. It is more harmful to use faculty with inadequate training to teach an object-oriented programming course than an imperative one. We need to make sure that experienced faculty are used in these foundation courses. Rather than accommodate all student demands for programming courses, we should reduce section offerings if qualified faculty are not available.

Under emphasis on modelling and theory

In the courses there is often a focus on syntax details and getting programs to run, not on problem solving, information modelling, understanding and reasoning about programs. So, programming and problem solving are still taught as an ad-hoc art without any underlying theory. Teaching focuses on individual languages and tools rather than giving the student a unified view of programming as a discipline. Instructors in later courses complain that their students cannot program.

Laboratories

Despite recommendations by ACM and ITiCSE working groups on laboratories for closed (i.e. supervised) laboratories, many schools use open laboratories. In many schools, students are still working without direct supervision. This is because of a lack of resources (instructors, computers, and space). In many cases, this leads to plagiarism, which is widespread in many countries.

Lack of women in Informatics courses

The percentage of women students in Informatics remains small. To some extent, this is because women tend to be intimidated by their male peers who spend more time on the computer playing games and surfing the Web. This leads women to form the incorrect belief that they will be at a disadvantage in a programming course, so they avoid taking a course for majors and enroll in a "terminal course" instead.

3. TRENDS

3.1 Paradigm shift

A paradigm shift from imperative to object-oriented problem solving is under way in many countries. Currently there are a number of approaches of how best to change from imperative to object-oriented thinking. There is also a trend away from text-based (e.g. "Hello World") programs to more student-oriented ones, because text-based examples do not motivate students of the multimedia generation. Problem-based learning approaches are becoming more popular in an increasing number of universities. Interdisciplinary projects (less lecture-based, more problem-based) and teamwork with students in other disciplines are also becoming more prevalent. Teamwork and collaborative learning in general are increasingly encouraged at an early stage.

3.2 Use of software development tools

Software engineering techniques (e.g. graphical modelling languages) for "programming in the large" are becoming more popular in introductory programming courses. There is an effort towards more rigorous software development and this includes teaching students how to prepare more and better documentation. A number of commercial and free software development tools are also in use to make students familiar with professional environments at a very early stage in their education. Tools, which generate code from user-specified object properties and class relationships, support this process, because students easily can see the advantage of the models they constructed beforehand.

On the other hand, the suitability of such professional environments for the learning process is being discussed. The most well known point of criticism is that their user interfaces with the huge variety of offered functions are optimized for efficient and fault-free software development, and not for learning software engineering. Moreover, these interfaces often guide users to avoid certain kinds of errors so they cannot learn from these errors. Thus, special educational versions with reduced functionality are used in some cases.

3.3 Visualization, animation and exploration

There is an increasing use of environments for the visualization of basic modelling and programming techniques, algorithm animation and program visualization. Online tutors and tools for the exploration of concepts are used for learning programming. An increasing number of these tools is available for free on the World Wide Web. We need to have mechanisms in place to verify the quality of free software tools. We must keep in mind that the initial price of software is a small part of the total cost (often free software requires maintenance and support).

3.4 Patterns and generic programming

To learn reuse, good design, and the experience of experts, learners are introduced to patterns and generic programming techniques (e.g. templates) in solution design and implementation.

4. CHALLENGES

Because of the rapid pace of change in Informatics, we need to find ways to keep educators up to date. Universities and Informatics Societies, industry and governments should devote resources to install mechanisms whose purpose it is to keep the faculties up to date. An approach used in Germany to enhance the theoretical foundation of Informatics education was to form departments for "Didactics of Informatics".

In teaching programming and problem solving, we face the following challenges:

- Teaching and learning programming is quite a difficult task. How can we teach programming without overwhelming the students with too many concepts at the same time? What concepts should be taught at each level (e.g. inheritance in the first or second course)? What does the programmer of the future have to know and what not?
- Faculty need to become more familiar with research that has been done to determine attributes for success in programming. We need to find ways to identify students who have these attributes and to encourage them to take programming courses. We need to be flexible in our teaching methods and teach students in ways that help them succeed.

- What will be the granularity level? How do we prepare our students to deal with the different granularity levels of programming?
- What is the best way to shift from the current programming paradigm to the next one? Although Java appears to be the primary teaching language today, that will likely change in the future.
- How do we accommodate diverse populations of students? How do we keep attrition rates low and maintain quality in our courses? How do we increase the number of women who take and complete the introductory programming courses?
- Modelling and programming languages and their libraries are becoming increasingly complex. How do we find a suitable subset for teaching purposes and how can we build up educational software libraries?
- How can we effectively use educational software libraries? Can metaphors and mini worlds be used effectively to teach introductory programming and if so, how?
- How do we make better use of visualization and exploration tools in teaching programming and problem solving? How do we develop such tools?
- Students should be able to see the commonalities between different paradigms and use concepts, where they are needed. Should we, and if so how should we, give students a broader view of programming, in which different paradigms are seen as different facets of a uniform framework?
- Although concurrency is increasingly present, there is no perceivable trend to introduce concurrent programming in first courses. Instead, the concurrency of programs is hidden from the user in various ways (e.g. event handling in Java programs). Should concurrency be included in the introductory sequence and if so, how?
- Multi-language programming is widely prevalent in industry today. How do we prepare our students to move easily towards multi-language programming?
- Because programming is more taught as a craft than as a science we should find ways to encourage a theoretical foundation for programming which is useable by practicing programmers and not only by mathematicians.
- In many institutions, the first programming sequence seems to be driven by short-term industrial demands (for example, what language does local industry need at the moment), rather than what may be best for the students in the long term. We need to find ways to find the right balance between pedagogical and industrial needs, so that we can do what is best for our students. We also need to be vigilant that the latest developments in the IT industry do not overly influence the direction of our courses.

- Currently the emphasis is on writing programs. We should teach students to write readable programs and to become more proficient in program reading.
- Research shows that active learning is more effective than passive learning. How do we incorporate active learning into introductory programming courses? One approach would be to implement problem-based learning as is currently being done in various engineering disciplines.
- Closed introductory programming laboratories require additional space. Institutions need to reallocate space from areas that have a surplus to Informatics.

5. FUTURE DIRECTIONS

We observe the following changes, which Informatics education has to address:

- Informatics is becoming more and more a mandatory subject in secondary education. An important question there is what aspects of Informatics should be common knowledge for all citizens of our society. The answer to this question will have a significant effect on how computing is taught in higher education.
- Perhaps because of the continued growth of Informatics education and subsequent pressures on students, plagiarism is a growing problem that we have to solve.
- Programming is undergoing fundamental changes. It is becoming more net-centric and multimedia-centered. These changes are driven by the increasing use of computing in all areas of society, not just text-based information processing. Traditional text-based programming education is not sufficient to address these changes.
- There is increasing demand from other disciplines to incorporate aspects of Informatics into their own curricula. We cite bio Informatics and computational linguistics as particular examples, but the demand comes from nearly all disciplines. Informatics is continuing to move away from its roots in scientific computation to infiltrate the whole range of disciplines.

Computing: The Shape of an Evolving Discipline

Lillian (Boots) Cassel [USA] (Co-Chair), Gordon Davies [UK] (Co-Chair), Deepak Kumar [USA] (Rapporteur)

Participants

Ralf Denzer [Germany], Anneke Hacquebard [The Netherlands], Richard J. LeBlanc Jr. [USA], Luiz Ernesto Merkle [Brazil], Fred Mulder [The Netherlands], Zeljko Panian [Croatia], Ricardo Reis [Brazil], Eric Roberts [USA], Paolo Rocchi [Italy], Maarten van Veen [The Netherlands], Avelino Francisco Zorzo [Brazil]

Abstract: The task of defining a computing curriculum that has wide international application is a difficult one. Defining a common core among computing disciplines is complicated by the continuing growth of more diverse sub-disciplines within computing and connections to a wider array of fields. The question whether we will be able to create a common understanding of excellence in our discipline is crucial for the quality of our education. In this report, we present an analysis of the current state of computing curriculum design and propose the development of a standard framework for looking at computing curricula, which could be used worldwide. For this purpose, a large-scale, multi-national effort will be necessary.

1. INTRODUCTION

The task of defining a computing curriculum that has wide international application is a difficult one. Despite the breadth that exists in recent international curriculum reports [3, 7, 12], that diversity is easily surpassed by the enormous variation found in the programs of study that currently exist in various universities throughout the world. Defining a common core among computing disciplines like computer science, information systems, computer engineering, software engineering, and so forth is complicated by the continuing growth of more diverse sub-disciplines within computing and connections to a wider array of fields. The working group discussed these issues and arrived at the following two important problems that are of immediate concern:

1. Can we develop a process for reviewing and analysing new programs of study proposals and curriculum recommendations against some established standards?
2. Are there ways to compare curriculum recommendations and find commonalities and distinctions across national boundaries?

These questions pose urgent concerns in the wake of the delivery of several extensive curricular definition reports and others that will be delivered in the near future. In this report we outline the current state and trends in curriculum development as well as the challenges being faced, and we make recommendations for future directions that focus on these questions.

2. CURRENT STATE

In recent years, several important curricular design proposals have appeared in the literature, including the following:

- ICF-2000 (Informatics Curriculum Framework 2000) produced by IFIP by commission from UNESCO [12].
- CC2001 (Computing Curricula 2001) produced by ACM and IEEE-CS [7].
- Career Space (Curriculum Development Guidelines, New ICT Curricula for the 21st century) developed by a consortium of 11 major ICT companies within the European Union (EU)[3].

The above list is not exhaustive. Other curricular documents exist and more are under active development. These curricula are quite diverse, reflecting the enormous variations in educational systems and philosophies throughout the world [11, 13]. A historical synthesis of curricular recommendations based on the diversity of the discipline of computing is presented in [9]. The underlying motivations for the design of various curricula range from knowledge-based curricula at one end of the spectrum to competency-based curricula at the other. While a number of the curriculum development efforts intend to be widely useful, all reflect the environments in which they are produced. Thus, CC2001 displays a focus on the United States educational system and ICF-2000 and Career Space are largely European [3, 11, 13].

In addition to the curriculum definitions, there are also profile definitions that describe the variety of jobs available in the computing area [3, 6]. Several curricular evaluation procedures and benchmarks are also in existence, and more are in development (for example, see [4]). Like the curricular documents, these reports exhibit a wide range of international differences. Computing is a broad discipline that is increasingly difficult to define precisely. At the same time, the field has undergone a process of maturation over the past fifty years that allows curriculum designers to benefit from past experience.

3. TRENDS

The diversity of curricular recommendations clearly suggests that the discipline of computing continues to broaden its boundaries. Given the continuing rapid pace of advances in the discipline and the impact of computing on new and emerging disciplines and application contexts (for example, see [5] on a program on *enviromatics*), the domain of computing will continue to expand as its interaction with other disciplines increases.

National and cultural differences play an important role in the design of curricula. Despite these differences, we recognize that the curricular documents will play a defining role not only in the continents where they were designed, but also in several other international contexts. Already, there have been several instances of specific instantiations of curricula based on these recommendations in other countries [1, 10] with Computing Curriculum 2001 being used in Brazil and China.

In the EU, *the Bologna Declaration (http://europa.eu.int/comm/education/socrates/erasmus/bologna.pdf)* is starting to have an effect. The declaration focuses on changes in the university educational systems in European countries to enable the mobility of students and the workforce. The goal is to create, in addition to the traditional degrees, a structure that substantially matches the Bachelor's and Master's degree programs in other countries. Further efforts to broaden the mobility of students and workers are needed in the light of increased communication and relocation.

Despite the presence of specific curricular documents, there is a wide range of specific programs at various universities. An excessive number of degree program names within the domain of computing are found in the United Kingdom. While the problem is not as acute in other locations, the trend to more programs of study in computing is evident. Such innovation is essential to maintain the vitality of the discipline, but it raises the longstanding issue of the identity of the field.

Given the diversity of degree programs operating under the umbrella of computing, the issue of accreditation becomes more challenging. In the US, accreditation criteria have evolved significantly from rigid but measurable guidelines to more flexible and institution-centred evaluation. In the UK, a new quality assurance system based on the idea of benchmarks is being implemented [4, 8] and the British Computer Society is incorporating the benchmark for Computing in to their accreditation process. In both cases, accreditation is increasingly outcome-oriented, although some countries continue to use more quantitative standardized metrics. New accreditation guidelines have to be developed for universities in the EU because of changes being brought about by *the Bologna Declaration.* These developments are perceived as encouraging signs of increased cooperation, especially in the European context, such as the ECTS (European Credit Transfer System) approach.

4. CHALLENGES

Perhaps the biggest challenge facing the community is to improve the understanding of various curricular recommendations and promote stronger cooperation among international communities. The goal of such an effort is to approach international applicability of various curricula. While some international communities have taken upon themselves to interpret and adapt already published curricula, we are also aware of resistance to adaptation in many other countries. We recognize that the existing curricular documents are a product of extensive research and substantial resources. Moreover, while most reflect a bias toward the educational systems of the countries in which they evolved, these curricula are excellent and comprehensive documents that can serve as a basis for defining curricula for other countries. We believe it is imperative to establish means for enabling comparison of curriculum recommendations and finding commonalities and distinctions across national boundaries. Can we develop a process for reviewing and analysing new programs and curriculum recommendations against some established standards?

To answer this question, one of the first steps is to define the space that makes up the discipline of computing and characterise it in such a way as to accommodate its continuing evolution. Some of the salient elements of the characterizations will include:

- **Body of Knowledge:** The traditional starting point in curriculum design is to identify the knowledge areas required for that discipline. The body of knowledge must specify the critical topics along with specifications of pre-requisites and desired student outcomes.
- **Foundational Material:** Within each subdiscipline it is important to identify the foundational material that represents the core knowledge of that curriculum. This foundational material has long term relevance for the field and will remain important for many years.
- **Application Context:** While computing related content remains important within the narrow confines of building better computers, languages, operating systems and other artifacts of the computing environment, computing is also a significant part of many application domains. Partnerships among disciplines are essential to solve a variety of problems in every field of human endeavor. Curricula that address these needs must bring together essential elements from many disciplines as integrated parts of a single goal.
- **Social Context:** The social context of a curriculum is affected by cultural and economic conditions and can have a profound effect on the structure and approach of its presentation.
- **Breadth and Depth:** As the field continues to broaden, curriculum proposals must balance the breadth of the field with the inclusion of the required depth.
- **Thematic Coherence:** For every new program that is proposed, it is important to establish that the program makes thematic sense and that its goals are coherent and well established and not necessarily driven by market forces and transient trends
- **Outcomes:** Any curriculum proposal must be able to define the desired set of characteristics that its graduates must possess after completing the program. The specification of competencies of graduates must be sufficiently fine grained so that they can be combined in various ways to describe different types and levels of qualifications.

Each of these elements will have both quantitative and qualitative components. While it is important to identify measurable assessment strategies, one cannot ignore the qualitative aspects of curriculum design. It is also important to ensure that the definition of the space incorporates proper professional and social contexts rather than just the list of topics that traditionally comprise the body of knowledge.

The accommodation and definition of new fields within computing should be facilitated to ensure sufficient transparency between curricula across national boundaries. We recognize that the dynamics of the discipline are different from other disciplines, especially as the discipline is starting to mature. We must attempt to take advantage of advances in pedagogy and also increase the level of interaction with appropriate stakeholders (that may include segments of industry as well as academic institutions in different countries). The process must also account for evaluation criteria that would facilitate explicit inclusion of issues surrounding diversity [2].

5. FUTURE DIRECTIONS

Defining ways to evaluate proposed curricula will require international cooperation. To define the space of valuable computing programs will require merging several existing bodies of knowledge. This would explicitly address the issues of competencies, the extensibility of the body of knowledge, the activities and experiences that would be a part of the curriculum, and the diversity of learning environments and delivery mechanisms that may be employed.

In an outcomes-based program evaluation, judgment must include an understanding of the result of an implementation the curriculum. Results can be expressed as profiles of graduates of the program that implements a particular curriculum recommendation. A profile may be related to a particular job description or to preparedness for further study in the field. The profile will consist of a set of competencies that are acquired through study and through experiences. Study is directly related to a body of knowledge and includes activities such as reading, discussion and practical work. The effect of study is demonstrated through examinations and other signs of accomplishment such as written reports or articles and presentations in various media. Experiences and activities are relevant to learning to use the body of knowledge in some context. These include laboratory activities, projects that require problem analysis, solution design and solution implementations. Relevant experiences can be achieved through class assignments, through internships and apprenticeships.

The process of curriculum evaluation should address different levels of outcomes based on student performance: threshold, modal, and top. A curriculum whose definition only addresses education for the average student will not include materials for developing the best students to their full potential. Thus, a fully developed curriculum will be expected to provide evidence of offering adequate opportunities for students at different levels. Students who perform at the topmost levels will receive appropriate challenges and opportunities to achieve competencies beyond those accessible by most students

There will be a need for several analysis tools to provide different ways of comparing programs to establish their strengths and weaknesses. These tools will include lists of topics from an extensible body of knowledge, competencies from which relevant profiles can be derived, experiences and activities that map topics to competencies, and ways of combining these elements and verifying that various conditions for consistency have been met. Such conditions will include the proper ordering of topic areas and experiences to assure that appropriate preparation precedes expected accomplishment; and evaluation of topic sets and experience to assure that sufficient breadth and depth are provided and lead to a meaningful profile. For example, the GRIP project is a comprehensive attempt at mapping job profiles with curricular descriptions [6]. Exploring such a process should be carried out at an international level to tap the expertise and experiences currently applied to different, but complementary projects. We expect this work to be carried out in a joint international project that combines efforts from many countries. While largely unifying in its goals, the project must be cognizant of national preferences, recognizing that curricula implementation will always take into account the local context and the experiences being provided to students using a wide variety of learning methodologies and environments.

6. SUMMARY

The answer to the question "Will we be able to create a common understanding of excellence in our discipline?" is crucial for the quality of our education. This can be achieved by developing a standard framework for looking at computing curricula, which could be used worldwide. For this purpose, a large-scale effort combining existing approaches is necessary.

In order to promote the health and benefits of the application of computing, it is essential to harness the energies and experiences of leaders in computing education around the world to produce a systematic method for comparing and merging curricular efforts and for assessing the potential contributions of proposed programs of study.

7. REFERENCES

[1]   Alvarez, J.: Innovations in Objectives, Content, Methodology and Grading in a First and Massive Computing Course, Keynote talk at of IFIP ICTEM 2002. Brazil, 2002.

[2]   Blank, D., Kumar, D.: Patterns of Curriculum Design, Proceedings of IFIP ICTEM 2002, Brazil, 2002.

[3]   Career Space: Curriculum Development Guidelines/New ICT Curricula for the 21st Century: Designing Tomorrow's Education, available on the worldwide web at http://www.career-space.com and http://www.cedefop.gr, Office for Official Publications of the European Communities, CEDEFOP (European Centre for the Development of Vocational Training)/Career Space. 2001.

[4]   Computing Benchmark Standard, published by the UK Quality Assurance Agency, Gloucester, England, 2000. www.qaa.ac.uk

[5]   Denzer, R: A Computing Program for Scientists and Engineers: What is the core of Computing? Proceedings of IFIP ICTEM 2002, Brazil, 2002.

[6]   GRIP (Generic Referential ICT Profiles), available on the worldwide web at http://www.grip-project.nl.

[7]   IEEE-CS & ACM: Computing Curricula 2001: Computer Science Volume, available on the worldwide web at: http://www.acm.org/sigcse/cc2001, IEEE-CS/ACM, 2001.

[8]   McGettrick, A.: Benchmark Standards for Computing in the UK, Proceedings of IFIP ICTEM 2002 (IFIP Working Group 3.2 Conference on Informatics Curricula, Teaching Methods and Best Practice), Brazil, 2002.

[9]   Merkle. L. E., Mercer, R. E.: Variations in Computing Science's Disciplinary Diversity: The case of curricula recommendations, Proceedings of IFIP ICTEM 2002, Brazil, 2002.

[10] Moraes, F. G., Zorzo, A. F., Calazans, N. L. V.: Deriving Different Computer Science Curricula from a Common Core of Disciplines, Proceedings of IFIP ICTEM 2002. Brazil, 2002.

[11] Mulder. F., Lemmen, K., van Veen, M.: Variety in Views of University Curriculum Schemes for Informatics/Computing/ICT, Proceedings of IFIP ICTEM 2002. Brazil, 2002.

[12] Mulder, F., van Weert, T. [eds], ICF-2000: Informatics Curriculum Framework for Higher Education. Paris, available on the worldwide web at http://www.ifip.or.at/pdf/ICF2001.pdf UNESCO/IFIP, 2000.

[13] Roberts, E.: CC-2001 and the Challenge of Defining a Curriculum, Keynote talk at of IFIP ICTEM 2002. Brazil, 2002.

Author Index

ALVAREZ, J.	125	LISBOA, M.	125
BARBOSA, H.	115	MACOME, A.	115
BLANK, D.	77	MARIANI, A.	63
BRINDA, T.	13, 125	MARTINS, J.	115
CASSEL, L.	131	MC GETTRICK, A.	3, 115
DA SILVA, E.	115	MERCER, R.	87
DAVIES, G.	131	MERKLE, L.	87, 131
DENZER, R.	69, 131	MULDER, F.	97, 131
DE OLIVEIRA, C.	115	ORTH, A.	115
FERREIRA, A.	115	PANIAN, Z.	131
HACQUEBARD, A.	131	REINFELDS, J.	41, 125
HARIDI, S.	53	REIS, R.	131
HUGHES, J.	115	ROBERTS, E.	131
KAASBOLL, J.	115	ROCCHI, P.	131
KERN, V.	115	SADAMANDA, R.	115
KOFFMANN, E.	21, 125	TORI, R.	115
KUMAR, A.	29, 125	VAN ROY, P.	53, 125
KUMAR, D.	77, 131	VAN VEEN, M.	97, 131
LE BLANC, R.	131	WAZLAWICK, R.	63, 125
LEMMEN, K.	97	ZORZO, A.	131

IFIP INTERNATIONAL FEDERATION
FOR INFORMATION PROCESSING 230
October 2002, 396 pp.
Hardbound, ISBN 1-4020-7219-8
EUR 184.00 / USD 175.00 / GBP 118.00

TelE-Learning

The Challenge for the Third Millennium

Edited by
Don Passey *Dept. of Educational Research, Lancaster University, UK*
Mike Kendall *Northamptonshire County Council, Northampton, UK*

TelE-LEARNING: The Challenge for the Third Millennium provides details of the most recent advances in this area, and covers issues concerned with:
■ the position of on-line learning in the development of the information society;
■ developments in virtual organisations, virtual institutes and virtual laboratories;
■ creation and development of interactive and adaptive context-aware learning environments using intelligent agents and cognitive style match;
■ integrating collaborative learning and collective competencies into on-line learning practices;
■ creation and development of e-learning portals, and concerns with inter-operability;
■ uses of on-line learning environments in diverse subjects, such as environmental education, mathematics and ICT;
■ changes with educational organisation and the impact of culture and culturation;
■ the role of case studies and models in teacher development of practice;
■ educational uses of broadcasting and web-based technology;
■ creation and development of assessment and computerised examination systems in on-line learning environments;
■ the role of team work, team learning and team teaching in on-line learning environments used for work-based purposes;
■ the role of on-line learning environments in parent-child relationships and rehabilitation situations;
■ a focus on shifts in female enrolment in computer science courses;
■ theories and concepts of telE-learning (including the application of activity theory and situated learning theory to on-line delivery and learning);
■ developments in appropriate research methodologies for on-line learning environments.

Contact information:
Customers in Europe, Middle East,
Africa, Asia and Australasia
Kluwer Academic Publishers,
P.O. Box 989, 3300 AZ Dordrecht,
The Netherlands
E orderdept@wkap.nl

Customers in USA, Canada,
Mexico and Latin America
Kluwer Academic Publishers,
101, Philip Drive, Assinippi Park,
Norwell, MA 02061, USA
E kluwer@wkap.com

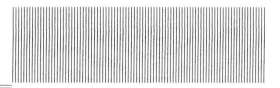

kluwer
the language of science

IFIP INTERNATIONAL FEDERATION
FOR INFORMATION PROCESSING 217
August 2002, 1032 pp.
Hardbound, ISBN 1-4020-7132-9
EUR 190.00 / USD 175.00 / GBP 120.00

Networking the Learner:
Computers in Education

Edited by
Deryn M. Watson *School of Education, King's College London, UK*
Jane Andersen *IT University of Copenhagen, Denmark*

The book is derived from selected contributions to the Seventh World Conference on Computers in Education (WCCE), which was sponsored by the International Federation for Information Processing (IFIP) and held in Copenhagen, Denmark in July/August 2001.
Networking the Learner: Computers in Education is presented in three parts:
■ Papers organised around themes: open and distance learning, ICT in learning, new pedagogic ideas, teaching mathematics, teaching computer science, forms of assessment, management and resources, teacher education, and national initiatives;
■ Professional groups providing reflections and perspectives on issues from social and ethical concerns, virtual universities, and the next generation of programming languages, to the interface between virtuality and reality in schools, and the role of large multi-national projects to stimulate change.
■ Reports of the lively discussions during panel sessions, such as provoking new images of research and practices, experiences of e-learning and e-training, and the future platforms in educational technology.

Keywords provide readers with different conceptual slices that can be found across the chapters, such as collaborative learning, problem solving, cognition and interactions.
Teachers and lecturers, policy makers and researchers, learners and authors, educational technologists and curriculum developers will find here a wealth of insights that do justice to this important topic.

Contact information:
Customers in Europe, Middle East, Africa, Asia and Australasia
Kluwer Academic Publishers,
P.O. Box 989, 3300 AZ Dordrecht,
The Netherlands
E orderdept@wkap.nl

Customers in USA, Canada, Mexico and Latin America
Kluwer Academic Publishers,
101, Philip Drive, Assinippi Park,
Norwell, MA 02061, USA
E kluwer@wkap.com

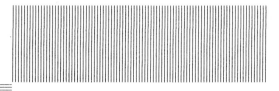

kluwer
the language of science

Pathways to Institutional Improvement with Information Technology in Educational Management

IFIP INTERNATIONAL FEDERATION
FOR INFORMATION PROCESSING 199

September 2001 , 180 pp.
Hardbound, ISBN 0-7923-7493-2
EUR 136.00 / USD 125.00 / GBP 86.00

eBook, ISBN 0-306-47006-3
June 2002
EUR 95.00 / USD 87.50

Edited by
C.J. Patrick Nolan , *Graduate School of Education, Massey University, Palmerston North, New Zealand*
Alex C.W. Fung, *Hong Kong Baptist University, Hong Kong SAR, PR of China*
Margaret Brown, *Graduate School of Education, Massey University, Palmerston North, New Zealand*

This volume presents findings and insights from contemporary thinking and research about alternative and new ways that computerised information systems might be designed and used to support the improvement of educational institutions. Many pathways are identified although expansion of access to and use of computerised systems by a much broader range of professionals than in the past is vital to the success of improvement initiatives. The contents are in four sections:

- Models for supporting and enhancing professional practice;
- Computerised school information system models and designs;
- Evaluation of system effects; and
- Making a difference through training and professional development.

Pathways to Institutional Improvement with Information Technology in Educational Management will be of interest to a wide range of educational professionals, researchers and system designers. The contents suggest, in particular, ways that educational professionals might revise their understandings of how computerised systems may in the future be designed and used to support key institutional processes, policy and strategy development, professional and executive decisions, and institutional planning and programme review. This book contains the selected proceedings of the Fourth International Working Conference on Information Technology in Educational Management, which was sponsored by the International Federation for Information Processing (IFIP) and held in Auckland, New Zealand, in July 2000.

Contact Information:

Customers in Europe, Middle East, Africa, Asia and Australasia:
Kluwer Academic Publishers
P.O. Box 989, 3300 AZ Dordrecht,
The Netherlands
E orderdept@wkap.nl

Customers in USA, Canada, Mexico, and Latin America
Kluwer Academic Publishers
101 Philip Drive, Assinippi Park,
Norwell, MA 02061, USA
E kluwer@wkap.com

kluwer
the language of science

Information and Communication Technologies in Education

The School of the Future

IFIP INTERNATIONAL FEDERATION
FOR INFORMATION PROCESSING 186
February 2001, 344 pp.
Hardbound, ISBN 0-7923-7298-0
EUR 190.50 / USD 165.00 / GBP 115.00

Edited by
Harriet Taylor, Louisiana State University, Baton Rouge, USA
Pieter Hogenbirk, CPS, Amersfoort, The Netherlands

Information and Communication Technologies (ICT) have already had a significant impact on education in many countries around the world. As the "Information Revolution" has an impact on world society, education is seen as a priority for the developed as well as the developing countries. It is an opportune moment to reflect on current practice and consider how schools can retain what is best, while changing to meet the needs and demands of the new world. This volume examines the many aspects of the integration of ICT into the school of the future. It describes the experiences of different countries in developing models of schools of the future with ICT at the foundation. It provides insights into the essential conditions for developing future new learning environments supported by ICT. It includes perspectives from both developed and developing countries as they prepare for future educational systems of the Information Age.

The main themes presented in this book are:

Experiences from a variety of national initiatives, policies, and strategies;
ICT tools for teaching and learning;
Distance and online learning;
Preparation of teachers for new ICT-rich learning environments;
Change and impact on learning of ICT;
The influence of ICT on school culture and organisation;
Cultural and historical perspectives;
Future perspectives for the use of ICT in schools.
This volume contains the selected proceedings of the International Conference on The Bookmark of the School of the Future, which was sponsored by the International Federation for Information Processing (IFIP) and held in April 2000 in Viña del Mar, Chile. Contributions from experts around the world make this volume an essential addition for professionals in the field of education, government, informatics and development.

Review(s)
`I enjoyed this book and will be recommending it for our library'
Computers & Education, 31 (2001)

Contact Information:

Customers in Europe, Middle East, Africa, Asia and Australasia:
Kluwer Academic Publishers
P.O. Box 989, 3300 AZ Dordrecht,
The Netherlands
E orderdept@wkap.nl

Customers in USA, Canada, Mexico, and Latin America
Kluwer Academic Publishers
101 Philip Drive, Assinippi Park,
Norwell, MA 02061, USA
E kluwer@wkap.com

kluwer
the language of science

Building University Electronic Educational Environments

IFIP INTERNATIONAL FEDERATION FOR INFORMATION PROCESSING 166

April 2000 , 296 pp.
Hardbound, ISBN 0-7923-7831-8
EUR 163.50 / USD 155.00 / GBP 107.00

Edited by
Stephen D. Franklin, *University of California, Irvine, USA*
Ellen Strenski, *University of California, Irvine, USA*

This volume contains selected papers and panel sessions from the International Working Conference on Building University Electronic Educational Environments, which was held at the University of California, Irvine, in August 1999, and was sponsored by the International Federation for Information Processing (IFIP) Working Groups 3.2 (Computers in University Education) and 3.6 (Distance Learning).

Together, these international perspectives range from the ultra-utilitarianism of skills training for employment to views traditionally characterized as representing a `liberal arts education.' Blending the immediately practical with more theoretical analyses, they probe the challenges of technology now confronting faculty, learners, and administrators alike, as all endeavor to understand and to exploit emerging opportunities while preserving the best of existing educational systems.

This book provides an historical benchmark, plots promising developments, and provides glimpses of possible futures.

Recurring themes and topics include:

National Plans and Projects;
Learning Paradigms;
Meeting Institutional Challenges;
Curriculum Development;
Defining and Building Technological Environments;
Scholarly Electronic Resources;
Lifelong Learning;
Better Learning Online.
This volume will be essential reading for IT researchers and professionals in higher education who are involved in building and using computing systems to realize a virtual university environment.

Contact Information:

Customers in Europe, Middle East, Africa, Asia and Australasia:
Kluwer Academic Publishers
P.O. Box 989, 3300 AZ Dordrecht,
The Netherlands
E orderdept@wkap.nl

Customers in USA, Canada, Mexico, and Latin America
Kluwer Academic Publishers
101 Philip Drive, Assinippi Park,
Norwell, MA 02061, USA
E kluwer@wkap.com

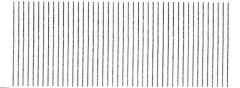

kluwer
the language of science

Communications and Networking in Education

Learning in a Networked Society

IFIP INTERNATIONAL FEDERATION FOR
INFORMATION PROCESSING 163
February 2000 , 352 pp.
Hardbound, ISBN 0-7923-7760-5
Printing on Demand
EUR 159.00 / USD 150.00 / GBP 103.50

Kluwer Academic Publishers is pleased to make this title available as a special Printing on Demand (PoD) edition. PoD books will be sent to you within 6-9 weeks of receipt of your order. Firm orders only: returns cannot be accepted as PoD books are only printed on request.

Edited by
Deryn M. Watson, *School of Education, King's College London, UK*
Toni Downes, *Faculty of Education, University of Western Sydney, Australia*

In most schools the dominant supporting technology has been either the stand-alone personal computer or a modest local network. The situation is changing rapidly as a rising number of schools provide access to the Internet for their staff and pupils, opening avenues for communication and networking hitherto not possible.

This book reflects on this change. It aims to further the vision of how these new technologies could improve and transform aspects of education. Yet in parallel it asks serious questions about the realities of an interface between the social, cultural and pedagogical contexts of education and the actual affordances that these new information and communication technologies offer.

Contact Information:

Customers in Europe, Middle East, Africa, Asia and Australasia:
Kluwer Academic Publishers
P.O. Box 989, 3300 AZ Dordrecht,
The Netherlands
E orderdept@wkap.nl

Customers in USA, Canada, Mexico, and Latin America
Kluwer Academic Publishers
101 Philip Drive, Assinippi Park,
Norwell, MA 02061, USA
E kluwer@wkap.com

The chapters in this book provide a heady mix of foresight and practical reporting, of planning for the future but at the same time respecting the problems education already has with current technologies. The richness of the points presented here stems in part from the range of experience of the international authors - from academics and administrators, to teachers and curriculum designers. This mix ensures that the central questions on communications and networking in education are considered not simply from a variety of personal perspectives, but also from different cultural and environmental experiences. And yet interest also lies in the commonality of reporting and discussion based on activity in the field. All the contributions draw heavily on research and experience in devising and running projects and experimental activities in a range of schools and teacher-training institutions and environments. The opinions expressed are thus grounded in knowledge gained from work embedded in the reality of today's educational settings. This must be the only sound base upon which to consider the issues of the future.

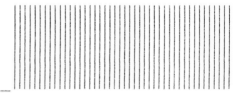

kluwer
the language of science